Shaktipat - The Miracle of Grace

Authentic Shaktipat, Who Can Give It,
The Benefits of Receiving It

By Kedarji

I0616312

Shaktipat - The Miracle of Grace
Authentic Shaktipat, Who Can Give It,
The Benefits of Receiving It

Copyright © 2025 by Kedarji

Copies of this book may be ordered by contacting:

The Bhakta School of Transformation, Inc.

330-623-7388 Ext. 10

NityanandaShaktipatYoga.org

ISBN: 979-8-218-66433-6

Printed in the United States of America

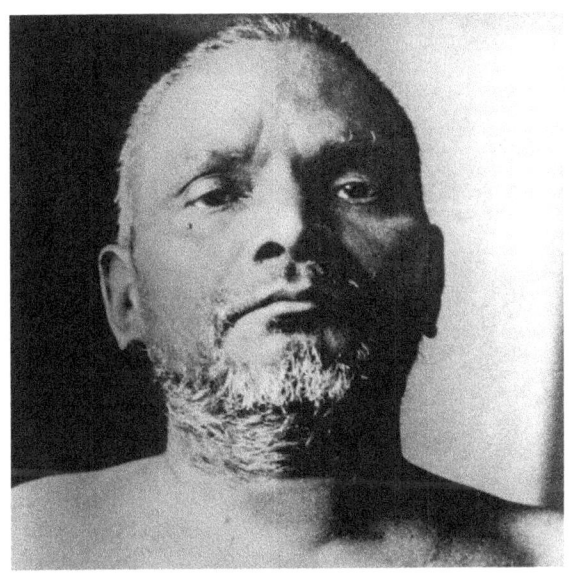

Shri Bhagawan Nityananda of Ganeshpuri
The Master of Kedarji's Lineage

Contents

Foreword

It appeared to be by chance that I met Kedarji. I say by chance because I wasn't technically seeking a Sadguru or a yogic path to deepen my spirituality. In all of the spiritual knowledge I had collected, I had never heard of a Sadguru or Shaktipat before. I was content to be a metaphysical junkie, following the hot new teachings of the day, pulling angel cards for guidance, carrying crystals for protection and meditating on positive affirmations – along with indulging the senses through visualization. This was my form of meditation.

In all of these things, the one thing I was seeking was to know the Truth. I wanted to know the Truth of my existence, the purpose of my life, and how to stop the suffering I experienced. I was looking to be happy.

Nothing happens by chance. That desire to know the Truth led me to cross paths with Kedarji. I had no idea I was to learn so much more than I thought was ever possible. A treasure was waiting for me that would begin with the Blessing of *Shaktipat*.

I was introduced to Kedarji through a mutual friend who asked if The Bhakta School of Transformation could hold a meditation program in my metaphysical education center. I happily agreed, as I was eager to experience the meditation he had to offer.

That cold December night, he walked through the door to my center wearing a vibrant smile and kind eyes. A sense of peace washed over me. I felt as if I had known him all my life.

Captivated by his talk on how to experience lasting inner peace, I leaned in to capture every word as if it would be the last time I would hear it. That night, he shared that the state of uninterrupted Bliss that he had attained, and that is attainable by each of us, was all due to the Blessing of Shaktipat and the journey that is *Sadhana*.

And then, to demonstrate his message, he led us through a meditation technique, that quieted my restless mind, in less than 3 minutes. My mind was actually quiet enough for me to notice the stark difference I had wrongly associated with my version of a quiet mind.

I was peaceful for the first time in a long time, meaning that I didn't drift back to thinking about my kids or list of chores. I was absorbed in a state of peace. This is what I had been seeking. I had never experienced this type of profound state before.

I could not argue with the experience I had just had. Here was an authentic Meditation Master, a being who was able to give me the direct experience of true meditation, and explain it in such a way that I, for the first time, understood the purpose of true mediation, which is to go beyond the mind and beyond the senses.

This experience was just the tip of the iceberg. I wanted to dive into that ocean of Bliss to see what wonders lay hidden just below the surface. So, I enrolled in a Weekend Shaktipat Blessing Retreat.

My experience of the receipt of Shaktipat in this retreat was very peaceful and subtle. My mind raced at first, full of thoughts and fears, but once my head was brushed with the peacock feathers, the restlessness stopped and I drifted into Bliss. *I experienced a state of awe and saw myself dive into an ocean and become one with it. From that point on in the experience, I was completely erased. There was no separation between me and the Supreme Intelligence.* I was shown who I really am. I was peaceful, content and happy like I had never experienced before. *It was a feeling I never wanted to end.* The true beauty of that experience was that I didn't cause that state of awe to happen. It was a Blessing of Kedarji's Grace. I could not have produced such an experience because I had no previous knowledge of such an experience and state of being!

My Shaktipat experience was a life changing experience but that was only the beginning. The meat of the experience came in the days following, when I entered into the *Shaktipat Kriya Process* that is also called Sadhana. This is where my life took on new meaning.

In this book, Kedarji shares that we have been going in the wrong direction for so many lifetimes. We are distracted and so very attached to worldliness that we cannot simply stop and change course without help. We don't know where we are or where to go.

For this reason, he talks about the subtleties of Shaktipat and the Shaktipat Kriya process that root out all the old bad habits that are not who we really are - the tendencies that keep us bound and stuck in suffering. He shares that the role of the Shaktipat Sadguru is to show us the root cause of our suffering and help us remove that cause. This is true healing. We start at the top, rather than the bottom.

Before I had received Kedarji's Shaktipat Blessing, I had no idea that I had any kind of mental conditioning, karmic impurities and bad habits that would be a driving force behind my behaviors, emotions and thoughts. At the time, I did not know that these tendencies are the influencing factor to my life's situations and circumstances.

Two days after receiving Shaktipat, through

the Grace of the Sadguru, I had an awareness, an inner knowing, wash over me, that I had a really bad habit of wanting to control and manipulate outcomes and people. I began to observe that every thought I held had some other motive subtly woven into it. I was positioning myself for the seat of control in everything I did. This awareness spoke to me in an indescribable way to where I had an understanding that I alone was responsible for the mess I was in. I was shown many situations where I engaged in this karmic tendency and how I pursued this to keep hold of my comfort, security and reward in life.

This process was showing me how I was being played by the karmic impurities known as the gunas and the malas, so I could stop reaching for them. I was flooded with emotions at having this realization. I was angry, sad, ashamed, in denial and yet deeply grateful at having been shown an obstacle in my path – the reason why I could not let go, heal and be happy. This Shaktipat Kriya Process is the easy means Kedarji speaks of. Ten years of seeking and practicing methods to gain this understanding was replaced in an instant. By this gift of Grace this experience carried me beyond my mind and senses in a way that was very spontaneous.

It is one thing to have the intellectual knowledge of these impurities, but how could I apply that? If left on my own to process this information I would surely fail. I have not seen the final destination nor do I know what pitfalls lie ahead of me. At best, I would be left with passing glimpses of peace. So, I chose Kedarji as my mentor and spiritual companion.

Sadhana requires leadership. We all need leadership to continue the journey to our primordial home, by engaging in the Shaktipat Kriya Process in the way that Kedarji shares in this book.

I won't give away all the gold in this foreword, but he uses brilliant analogies, from luxury ocean liners to cab drivers to flowers in a garden, to help us understand the importance of receiving Shaktipat. He expresses why there is the need to nurture this gift of Grace through the Shaktipat Kriya Process, along with the change in lifestyle that is required to do so.

Muktananda Paramahamsa, a great Siddha Guru in our lineage, has shared, "We do not meditate only to relax a little and experience some peace. We meditate to unfold our inner being." We unfold our inner being by the lifestyle change that is the means to help keep us get into the boat of Grace that will surely take us safely to the distant shore of the Self. Kedarji shares the means to make such changes, embodied in his 4 Pillars of Joy In Daily Living.

My reaching for this old bad habit of wanting to control and manipulate everything and everyone is being broken. This is due to Kedarji's spiritual leadership and the approach and practices laid out in *Nityananda Shaktipat Yoga*.

"Awake to the Supreme Intelligence! Your treasure awaits you. Claim it now. Don't waste any more time. You are so much greater than you think you are."
~ Kedarji

This is one of my favorite quotes from my Gurudev, Kedarji. When I read this, I am reminded of the unconditional Love he and all of the Spiritually-perfected masters of our lineage transmit to us. With great urgency *the time is now* for us to awaken to this most precious gift that begins with the Blessing of

Shaktipat.

Shaktipat - The Miracle of Grace - Authentic Shaktipat and Who Can Give It is a book that reveals the Truth about this Blessing in a very relatable and direct way. This book is an invaluable resource for the newcomer seeking to know more about Shaktipat and why the Shaktipat Kriya process is necessary for permanent spiritual transformation. The seasoned Yogi can also find useful reminders in these pages to rekindle the flame of self-effort and remember his or her intention for engaging in the journey of retracing one's steps back to God.

Deana Tareshawty
Vice President
The Bhakta School of Transformation

Introduction

In this book I use the names Siddha Guru, Shaktipat Guru, Sadguru, Shaktipat Siddha Guru, Shaktipat Sadguru and Master interchangeably. They are a reference to the same spiritual leader who transmits Shaktipat.

First, I want you to remember this: The Shaktipat Siddha Guru is equal to you in Divinity because God exists equally in everyone and everything, everywhere. So, Shaktipat Gurus are only different from you in one respect. They have attained that which you are seeking. Therefore, the difference is one of attainment, not of equality. Realizing the Self requires the developed ability to tap into and merge with that Divinity, that energy substratum of everything. Shaktipat Siddha Gurus have mastered this ability where others may not yet have done so. In this regard, the Siddhas - the true Gurus - simply want to make you like themselves in this unfolding mastery.

Now, just imagine starting at the top rather than the bottom. What is it like to start at the destination, rather than in search of the destination? *This is the easy means of authentic Shaktipat.*

The point of receiving Shaktipat is to engage the means to evolve so that you come to live in a state of Grace as a constant. This is a state of rapture so profound as to leave you in awe of everything and everyone, all the time. It is a state of constant, spontaneous inspiration. It is a state of permanent, lasting inner peace filled with indescribable Joy. *It is egoless.*

Love is the highest religion, the greatest spiritual path of humankind. Therefore, I welcome you with Love, I honor you and I respect you. Love is all there is. Grace is God's Love. The awakening into Pure Perceiving Awareness, Infinite Awareness of the

Highest that we refer to as Shaktipat is Love. The journey to recognition of our true nature is Love. Ours is an approach where we lead with Love. In the end, it all comes back to Love.

After the receipt of Shaktipat that is the full Kundalini awakening, leadership in Sadhana is required. This is so because all spiritual attainment must be tested. I know this may not be what you want to hear. However, consider this. How will you know that you have attained anything lasting and worthwhile if you are not tested? How will you come to know the difference between when it's your ego and restless mind talking and when it is God, the inner Self talking?

Of course, you already understand the importance of this kind of leadership in mundane matters. For example, if you got your education in the school and university system then you know that you did not and could not test yourself. You had a teacher, hopefully someone who was a great leader, who had the responsibility of giving you tests to determine whether or not you had learned the subject matter properly and applied it. This test was administered by the authority on the topic you studied. You were graded in order to determine your worth on the subject matter. If you got a failing grade and had a good leader in your teacher, you were offered a means of correcting your weaknesses on the subject and then you were retested. This is just one of several examples that can be offered.

In spiritual life, particularly under the tutelage of a Shaktipat Siddha Guru, it is no different. This is why you need the discipline offered through strong spiritual leadership. Strong spiritual leadership is one in which the leader leads by example, from direct experience of having mastered what is being taught.

Talk Is Cheap

There is a lot of talk these days about people experiencing higher states of Divine Consciousness, once thought to be rare and difficult to attain, with little or no effort. Many people have, therefore, become skeptical of claims of higher states of Divine Consciousness. And they should be in this regard.

Is it possible to have an epiphany, spiritual breakthrough or elevated awareness of God with no effort? Yes. These can come as glimpses, but glimpses are not lasting attainment. Therefore, any such experiences, if they are true experiences (meaning not filtered through the ego or mental conditioning of any kind), should be understood as a message to find the means and path to go higher, to become established in the Self.

Is This Witchcraft or Voodoo?!

Sometimes, when people hear the words Shaktipat, spiritual initiation and Guru uttered in the same breath, they are confused or even frightened. The many opinions on the Internet that are floated as facts don't make matters any easier.

The truth is we accept and undergo many initiations in life. For example, being welcomed and embraced by a fraternity or sorority in college often means undergoing an initiation. Many people have their children baptized and this is a widely accepted initiation, as is the ceremony of Holy Communion in the Catholic tradition.

Training in corporate communication and embracing the underlying culture at one's job also involves a certain initiation. Attorneys are initiated into the culture of their law firms and doctors are initiated into the mindset of the pharmaceutical companies whose product their prognosis often relies upon to treat symptoms of their patients.

What About All Those Rituals We Know and Accept?

Then there are the rituals that we perform every day, perhaps without recognizing them as every bit a ritual as the spiritual ceremony inherent in events like baptism and holy communion. For example, what we do and comply with to fast track a result in applying for a loan or a new job. Or rituals like coffee and croissants at Starbucks every morning at the same time, at the same table. Or rushing home to catch the next episode or a rerun of *Breaking Bad* – with the same martini in hand, stirred not shaken, and a lemon rind, not a lemon wedge, while sitting in the same spot in your recliner, not on the coach, at exactly 5 minutes before the start of the show, so that you can catch your favorite Capital One credit card commercial – what's in your wallet?!

These are each just examples of how we accept and fully embrace rituals and initiations in everyday life. The only difference between this and Shaktipat is that Shaktipat is an initiation that you may not be familiar with. And it is the initiation of all initiations!

Starting At the Destination

Shaktipat is the easy means to forming a powerful connection with the true YOU – your true nature, your most powerful aspect, your highest Self.

It is starting at the destination rather than climbing a ladder.

Think, for a moment, of the caffeine in coffee, which so many people drink precisely to get a boost, to fast-track the energy they need to get started with their day. Or, what about the music you listen to in order to lift your spirits, calm your tension or get you psyched/pumped to perform better?

We buy E-Z passes to fly through tollbooths, to fast-track our progress in getting from point A to point B with the greatest convenience, and without being held back or slowed down. We attempt to get security clearance passes for airline travel to fast-track getting on planes, or special access passes to ensure we get into our favorite concerts or sporting events with no waiting.

The Exception Here Is the Difference That Makes the Difference

Shaktipat is not like any other ritual or ceremony. It is the *easy means* to accessing your highest power, the power of Grace – The Spiritual Power that is your true nature – *the highest power that is the energy substratum of everything and everyone.* **Shaktipat initiation is like lighting an unlit candle with one that is already lit. In the leap of that flame, so much takes place – and in an instant!**

Shaktipat and Lineage

A Siddha Guru or Shaktipat Guru cannot continue to give Shaktipat based on storing up the maximum amount of Chit Shakti alone. If the Shaktipat is authentic it is because such a being relies upon the power of a lineage of such Gurus.

That power continues to flow through the

Shaktipat Guru from that lineage only if that Guru continues to please the lineage. This is why lineage is so important. One enters the lineage of his/her Guru when that Guru initiates him and then leads him/her in Sadhana. This is the only way to become fully established in the indescribable Joy of the Self that is the foundation for living in a state of Grace.

Through an authentic Shaktipat Guru, there is an experience that becomes permanent over a period of time of performing Sadhana under such a Guru. This experience can and does also happen for many, upon the receipt of Shaktipat. The restless mind becomes quiet, there is a steady experience of peace, the reason why love is supreme becomes evident and there is a growing experience of the Bliss of the Self.

There is a barrier that presents the greatest challenge to becoming established in a state of Grace. That barrier is our ignorance of the transcendental and immanent aspects of God, our ignorance of these two aspects being contained in each other, and in way that there are no boundaries between the two. The formless Absolute is God's transcendental aspect. The immanent aspect is this world appearance, full of forms.

The barrier in God's immanent aspect is, for many, expressed as attachment to the false notion of being just the body, the mind and the senses, just a person with a particular personality, a set of genes and so on. This is the barrier that, for permanent spiritual transformation to take root, must be erased.

In my experience and that of so many others, the easiest means to this is the bond of power between a living Shaktipat Guru who is the embodiment of the highest state, and the Devotee. Through such a being the power of that Guru's lineage, over time and with instructed practice, erases the barrier I just spoke of. Then, for the Disciple, there is no difference in experience between the outer physical form of the Guru and that Guru's subtle form inside.

Once this barrier has been erased something else begins to occur. The Siddhas - the Sadgurus of that Guru's lineage - begin to appear to the Devotee inside. Deities connected to the lineage also begin to appear inside the Devotee during meditation, chanting, contemplation and japa. In fact, this is one of the hallmarks of authentic Shaktipat – an indication that you're with the right one.

Lineage

An unbroken lineage can be a lineage of one Shaktipat Sadguru and his/her small group of Disciples who carry on the offering by his/her Guru's command. One example of this is a comparison between the Sage Vasishtha and the Guru Vishvamitra. Vishvamitra had thousands of devotees but produced no great spiritual leaders or Sadgurus. Vasishtha, on the other hand had very few devotees and produced one great Sadguru and spiritual leader. He gave the world Shri Rama. And how great that Rama (the subject of The Ramayana) is!

Or an unbroken lineage can be one in which there are Shaktipat Sadgurus in a long lineage of such beings. These are disciples who have been transformed by their own Guru, with the same blessing of Grace and instruction that other beings in the lineage have merged with and been transformed by.

This is *Parampara* – meaning that the lineage is kept alive by the passage of the Kula Dharma, handed down orally from Shaktipat Siddha Guru to Disciple, down through the ages. This is the case even if there appears to be a break in the chronological/historical order of the passage of leadership from one Guru to another, *because there is no inner break*. Also, in decades past in which we were not present, chronological/historical accounting of passage of a lineage often has to be accepted by inference because we don't always know how accurate the recording is.

I share this because there are a number of organizations and foundations that have experienced upheavals in their leadership upon the passing of a Sadguru in the lineage who was the spiritual head of that organization. Typically, the organization that is able to weather the storm of that upheaval, for a variety of reasons that usually include money at the top of the list, will then insist that they are the only body that can tell the public who and who is not a lineage holder of that Sadguru or who is and who is not a Siddha.

This often occurs even when the organization has no current knowledge of the being's offering whom they say is not a Sadguru, but just a person. This is an unfortunate phenomenon that has occurred far too often.

Organizations Do Not Make Shaktipat Gurus

What is important to understand is that organizations do not make Shaktipat Gurus. Only an authentic Shaktipat Guru in a lineage of such beings can make and authorize another Shaktipat Guru. If this were not the case, then an organization or group of people could also claim that it is their sole right to decide who is worthy and who is not, who is God and who is not.

Of course, this would make such an organization just like the early Catholic Church that carried out the crusades to force this kind of opinion on to people everywhere. History has taught us how dark a chapter in the existence of societies this was.

Having stated the importance of a lineage,

please use this link for more information about Kedarji's lineage in Nityananda Shaktipat Yoga. https://www.nityanandashaktipatyoga.org/our-lineage/.

I place my head at the lotus feet of my Shri Gurudev, *Muktananda Paramahamsa,* along with our Nityananda Shaktipat Yoga lineage who are entirely responsible for this work. The offering of the Shakti power of our lineage happened by way of the command received from the great Shri Bhagawan Nityananda of Ganeshpuri, the Master of our Shiva lineage in these modern times. This is a lineage of Shaktipat Siddha Gurus dating back to the pre-Bronze Age.

What If?

What if you could experience a state of peace and indescribable joy, while calming your restless mind in less than 3 minutes, without years of meditation practice? What if you could experience unconditional love and compassion for yourself and for others while, at the same time, experiencing a state of fearlessness beyond comparison, without years of arduous struggle?

In the early stages of my meditation practice (the first 10 years), I spent hours each day meditating vigilantly. I had spent a year studying with Zen monks in a Zen monastery. During that time, I was taught a form of Zen meditation. Later, I took up Transcendental Meditation under the supervision of an assigned meditation coach. At the same time, I had fervently examined many scriptures and sacred texts of the world's religious and spiritual paths. Many of these texts were ripe with utterances of Saints and Sages of the varying traditions embodied in those scriptures.

I spent enough time studying and reexamining

these to know that, in all my years of meditating, I had not had a single inner experience like the ones these Sages spoke of in their utterances! No visions of light and sound, no visitations of Saints past, no strong inner voice leading me - and no experiences of the indescribable Joy, the sweet Bliss that I had read about. The only experience I could look forward to at that time was being in "time out." I battled to make my restless mind quiet enough to have a momentary glimpse of peace.

This is the way it was until I met Muktananda Paramahamsa and received Shaktipat, along with being initiated into the great Shiva lineage of Bhagawan Nityananda of Ganeshpuri. https://bhagawannityananda.org/.

This blessing of Grace was authentic Shaktipat. Immediately, my meditations became spontaneous - with my mind stopping and dissolving at spontaneous intervals during meditation. I quickly began to have visions of Divine Light and wonderful inner sounds (celestial music).

I was given a Mantra that had a powerful impact on making my mind quiet. The chanting practice I was taught was a powerful form of Meditation unto itself. And the most important experience of all is that I finally attained states of indescribable Joy, *on a regular basis.* A state of peace washed over me, increasing my experience of content, gratitude and deeply heartfelt Love *without distinctions.*

And this was just the beginning. The Shaktipat Kriya Process that came afterward was the ultimate Blessing and journey to the permanent experience of the states I describe above. This is what *authentic* Shaktipat is all about.

Why Shaktipat?

To answer that question, here's a partial list:

- If you meditate now, you'll meditate better.
- If you don't meditate now, you'll be able to easily start a daily meditation, chanting and Mantra Yoga practice.
- You'll be set on a path to be happy for no good reason, *permanently*.
- You'll begin a process, *an unfolding* that will deliver you to lasting peace, indescribable joy, love without distinctions and the inner strength necessary to take on life's challenges with a smile on your face.
- You'll be set on a trajectory to well-being in all the areas of your life.

Most importantly, the Grace-bestowing power necessary to address and remove all the Karmic obstacles that keep you bound to fear, anxiety, doubt, worry, frustration, anger, lust, corruption due to greed, sarcasm and cynicism – this power of Grace comes by way of a Blessing that is transmitted to you. This begins a journey to an exalted state of well-being that is both incomparable and fulfilling in every way, by helping you get rid of all that you are not – those Karmas.

Your Effort

Will there be additional, extended effort and discipline required on your part? Yes. And, with Grace, what is required to resolve your identity crisis in favor of permanent spiritual transformation is easy to apply.

This point about Karmas is overlooked by so

many. We all have karmic baggage from so many past lives and the present life. These Karmas dictate our past and present mental conditioning *in a way that we come to love good news about our bad habits.* Once this particular bad habit becomes the norm, it's easy to get stuck in wanting a means that does not require that you work for the beneficial attainment.

This also leads to *mindless convenience* where you want everything fast, fast, fast – with no requirement for applied effort over an extended period of time. This is all due to Karmas. Once these karmas are removed, *That*, the Ultimate Reality, the inner Self comes looking for you. This is the power of the Blessing of Grace inherent in authentic Shaktipat.

The Greatest Gift

Shaktipat is the greatest spiritual initiation. After receiving it, a profound shift in my spiritual journey began very quickly. This happened within days of having this transmission of God's Grace bestowed on me. Later, I was taught about this being the first step in mastering Shaktipat Meditation and engaging what we refer to here in Nityananda Shaktipat Yoga as the *Shaktipat Kriya Process* or, simply, *Sadhana.* https://www.nityanandashaktipatyoga.org/.

I have received a number of 'initiations' in my life, some of them religious and/or spiritual (baptism as a baby, baptism in a river as a young adult, benedictions, American Indian initiation ceremonies and initiation into monastic life). But I had never experienced an initiation like this – one that was the greatest gift of my life – an initiation that spontaneously began an incredible, transforming journey of retracing my steps back to God.

Prior to receiving this blessing of Grace that also invoked healing on so many tangible levels, I had never had a personal relationship with God. I had never had the direct experience of the Absolute. My experience had been limited to intellectual knowledge with a few short glimpses of something 'other worldly' here and there. And my spiritual attainment (or lack thereof) had never been *tested*.

All of this changed under the spiritual leadership and companionship of my Shri Gurudev!

Chapter 1
Why Shaktipat Is Essential For
Permanent Spiritual Transformation

*"One must seek the shortest route and fastest means to
get back home, to turn one's inner spark into a blaze
and then to merge and identify with that greater fire
which ignited the spark."*
~ Bhagawan Nityananda of Ganeshpuri

Mazerunner

After receiving Shaktipat, as I took up my
Sadhana under the leadership of my Guru, I had a
huge realization. Up to that point, my entire existence
had been taken up with the following: Becoming
somebody in the eyes of others, pursuing comfort,
security and reward and mastering the ability to
manipulate and control outcomes by way of
possessing people, places and things on some level
and to some worthwhile degree. These made my
mind restless, wandering here and there like a mouse
looking for cheese.

My existence consisted of running a maze,
believing the cheese to be the ultimate reward. I was a
maze runner! What I did not realize at the time is that
when I got the cheese, I was still stuck in the maze. If
you put a mouse at the entrance of a maze, you can
train the mouse to run the maze until it finally gets
the cheese at the end of the maze. The mouse is then
entirely focused on eating the cheese, not even
thinking about how it will get out of the maze.

Only after eating the cheese does the mouse
even attempt to gain release from the maze. In most
cases, the mouse cannot find its way out of the maze

and gives up. The lab technician has to lift the mouse out of it.

I was like that mouse. Day after day I ran the maze of worldliness, chasing after notions and people, place and things - following the follower to become somebody in the eyes of others - hoping to possess people, places and things and desiring the comfort, security and reward that I perceived others had. It was the same playbook that most everyone else had - a playbook determined by the understandings hoisted on me by society, those I kept close to me, and the popular media I pursued defiantly. Sound familiar?

We live on a rock that hangs in a void of space, with no material support, while spinning on an axis in an orbit around a fireball.

No nation, no government, no world leader or dictator, no army or group of people anywhere and no criminal or organized crime group and none of the financially wealthy has any control over this.

Further, there is a distinct, verifiable order in how the movement of this realm takes place, day in and day out, for millennia. The Sun rises and sets at an appointed time that we cannot influence or change. And so it is for the moon, as well. Wind blows and ceases, rivers and oceans rise and fall, species come and go, and we are all subject to birth and death of the body. And who decided that females will bear children, rather than males? I think you get my point.

There is a sacred law here that supersedes all societal law. Wherever there is law, there is a *lawgiver.* So, it is very relevant, both for permanent spiritual transformation and overall well-being that we begin our journey by discovering and experiencing who or what this lawgiver is, along with our relationship to this lawgiver.

Of the Mind Only

Everything I've described above with respect to the maze begins with the mind. The mind is a contracted form of the same energy that has brought this entire cosmos into being. So, your mind has great power. The restless mind never stops weaving new worlds into being. This restlessness causes you to be bound in the pursuit of both pleasure and pain. Pleasure and pain are contained in each other. So, the pursuit of one inevitably leads to pursuit of the other.

But all of this is of the mind only. This is easily observed by going beyond your mind and beyond your body and your senses to that witness to your mind. That witness, that observer or indweller is who you really are. This is experienced by way of Witness Consciousness where you are able to operate from the experience of the observer, in order to expand your spiritual witnessing awareness of everything and everyone.

Shaktipat is the first, essential step to making the restless mind quiet in order to *permanently* increase your spiritual witnessing awareness. It is the easy means to this end that also sets the stage for the journey to permanent spiritual transformation that is ripe with the indescribable Joy of the Self, and the fearlessness to embrace that Joy. *Shaktipat is the essential first step for permanent release from the maze.* It is the foundation for what we refer to in Nityananda Shaktipat Yoga as the 4 Pillars of Joy In Daily Living.

Everyone wants to be happy, healthy and wise. Therefore, the challenge is people seek these where they are not – like searching for water in a desert when you live by an ocean. The restless mind and the attachment to body, mind and senses is overwhelmingly strong for most people. This attachment always brings suffering, and this predicament is due to one's past and present karmas. You cannot destroy these karmas with worldly methods, no more than you can pull yourself up into the air by your own bootstraps.

The full Kundalini awakening is the initiation that opens the floodgates of Grace necessary to destroy all the karmic obstacles to inner Peace, Joy and the ocean of God's Love, in a way that ends your seeking. This Grace comes from a master and the Shaktipat Blessing has proved to be the spark that ignites permanent spiritual transformation and lasting well-being in every area of life.

Those who receive Shaktipat here in Nityananda Shaktipat Yoga are able to easily attain higher and higher states of lasting spiritual awareness while, at the same time, improving their daily mundane lives for well-being and vibrant health.

Your Pot of Karmas

If you have a consistent itch on your face, or an unexplained lump on your lip, how do you begin to determine what's actually taking place on your face? *You look in a mirror.* You need the agency of a mirror to see your face, to reflect the spot where the itch and/or lump is, in such a way that you can further examine it to determine whether it's just passing acne or something more serious – so that you can address it to stop the itching and any underlying cause. Without a mirror to reflect your face, you're simply shooting blind.

Imagine treating an itch on your face with a Swiss army knife, attempting to carve it away by bludgeoning your face, when all that was needed was to wash away the dirt causing the itch! And all because you didn't have a mirror with which to see the spec of dirt that simply needed to be washed away with some warm water! The suffrage of your Karmas is just like this.

"A blind person may hold a light in his hand, but that light is of no use to him."
~ Shri Bhagawan Nityananda of Ganeshpuri

This profound utterance of Bhagawan Nityananda really does sum up why the right understanding of Shaktipat, *as a Grace-filled process that one is led through*, is so necessary to experience and imbibe authentic Shaktipat. I have met many people claiming to have received Shaktipat from their boyfriends, lovers, wives and 'spontaneous awakenings.' In observing such people over an extended period of time, I have seen that they have no lasting attainment. Whatever they think they received has become either a distant memory or a vicarious glimpse relived at the behest of the doership of the ego. Such people would do well to contemplate my Shri Nityananda's utterance.

We all have many Karmas, accumulated over many past lives and the present life. The storehouse of Karmas is inconceivably vast. It is only by the Grace, Blessing and leadership of a Siddha Guru who is a Shaktipat Guru in a lineage of such beings that we can even begin to understand and experience this Truth. Furthermore, it is only by such a being's Grace that these Karmas can be destroyed. This is why Shaktipat is essential for permanent spiritual transformation. And this is why I took a Shaktipat Guru and obeyed His every instruction and command.

"The ego is like a black bug on a black rock on a moonless night. How can you even hope to see it without the light of the living Master's Grace?"
~ The Poet Saint Kabir

The false notion of individuality that gives rise to the ego-idea is one of many Karmic tendencies that are embodied in the impurities embedded in our subtle body – *the world of our inner impressions.* We refer to these impurities using their scriptural terms from the Vedas and Shaiva Agamas. They are known as the three Gunas and the three Malas. The Gunas and the Malas are impurities that manifest as the embodiment of our Karmas in the many ways in which they have been expressed over countless lifetimes.

These impurities are actually planted in our being by God, to drive us back to Oneness with the Self. This is part of the extraordinary play of Divine Consciousness that rules this place. It may seem illogical, harsh or even cruel that a just, compassionate God would create useless contraction in binding, karmic tendencies. But consider this as an example: How does a long distance hurdler training for competition become a champion? Because great runners who are hurdlers *are not born that way.* They train for many years. I know because I used to run hurdles as an Olympic athlete in training.

The hurdles are the *necessary obstacles* that cause the hurdler to get stronger and stronger in running the hurdles. Without those *obstacles,* the runner cannot get strong enough to compete. So, the obstacles in the hurdles themselves are an absolute necessity, both in the training of the runner *and in the testing of the runner's attainment and preparedness for competing.*

Similarly, in Sadhana, *we understand the play of the Gunas and the Malas – these karmic impurities – to be just like those hurdles.* In fact, the mantra 'Guru' actually means the one who first takes you to and shows you the darkness of these impurities. Only then does the Guru then open your eyes so that you can actually see and begin to understand, experience and fully embrace the light you hold in your hand – your unclaimed treasure within.

So, without being led through an authentic process where the ways in which you conceal that glowing inner light from yourself (due to your Karmas) are revealed, you are just like that blind man that Bhagawan Nityananda speaks of - with a light in his hand that is useless to him because he can't see it.

"Guru Janam Janam Ki Atak Kholi" is a quote of the poet saint Kabir. It means that the Shaktipat Siddha Guru has freed you from being stuck for so many lifetimes. My own Guru used the following analogy. Before CDs there were LPs. These were long-playing records made from petroleum and were played on a phonograph that used a needle to play the sound in the grooves of the LP. Sometimes that needle would get stuck in one of the grooves, playing the same section over and over again, until someone came and lifted the needle from the groove. The Shaktipat Guru is the one who lifts the needle that is stuck in the groove of your karmas.

Receiving Shaktipat and engaging in the instruction for daily spiritual practice after the receipt of Shaktipat gradually delivers you to a state of being free from fear, anxiety, doubt, worry, sarcasm, cynicism, greed, anger and lust. You become happy and free. What's wrong with that!?

The 4 Pillars of Joy In Daily Living

Integrated into the *Nityananda Shaktipat Yoga* curriculum that is taught in our school is what I call the 4 pillars of Joy In Daily Living. These 4 pillars help to frame the journey back home embodied in what Shaktipat really is. They are the foundation for the daily spiritual practices that define why Shaktipat is essential for permanent spiritual transformation. They are:

1. The Spiritual Power
2. An Improved Mental State
3. Emotional Resilience
4. Vibrant Health

The Spiritual Power

The Spiritual Power is the first and foremost of the 4 Pillars of Joy In Daily Living that frame the Nityananda Shaktipat Yoga practices. In our experience, without this first pillar, it is impossible to experience permanent spiritual transformation in the long-term. So, as did my Shri Gurudev, *we define spiritual transformation as having a very strong foundation in The Spiritual Power.*

The Spiritual Power is that power that reveals our true identities, our Oneness with the lawgiver. 'Light bulb' is a name given to a piece of glass fashioned with metal pieces inside it, and a metal base as a connector. The name is really an oxymoron because, even though the light bulb is paraded around as the light source for our environmental living, indoors and out, *light bulbs do not give off light.* **It's the electricity, the power source that gives the light**. The light bulb is just a conductor that has to be connected to that power source in order to transmit light.

In true spirituality, it is the same. The physical body, the mind, the senses – these cannot function on their own. *They have no agency of their own.* They require power - energy with which to function. In one way, you already know this. Because when that power, that energy substratum leaves the body, you call that death. And no one has any interest in a dead body. The body is only attractive and embraced, to one degree or another, due to the power that resides inside it. Once that energy leaves the body, that body, the mind, the brain, the senses – these become inert and worthless!

Therefore, in our approach, this energy substratum of all things, the *Shakti*, is accessed, experienced and nurtured by using time-honored, effective methods proved to help you go beyond your mind, body and senses to experience, nurture and embrace that highest Power that is also the lawgiver here. You'll notice that I said, "Accessed." This is a power that you already possess. It cannot be given to you nor taken away from you. It is the power that contracts to become your mind, your senses, etc. *It is the power source for everything else.*

So, the only true spiritual methods, the only true spirituality is that approach which provides us with the methods and pathway to experience and embrace this *Spiritual Power*, out of which naturally and spontaneously (not to say without effort, but with tremendous inspiration and intuition) flow an *Improved Mental State*, the second pillar, *Emotional Resilience*, the third pillar and *Vibrant Health of the physical body*, the fourth pillar.

In order to recognize, experience and embrace our Oneness with this Spiritual Power, *we need an ever-increasing Awareness of it*. We refer to this as spiritual or witnessing awareness and it is by this awareness that we come to realize and identify with this Spiritual Power. *However, this spiritual awareness is asleep in us.* If we are fortunate enough to cross paths with a genuine Shaktipat Guru then this awareness can be fully awakened by way of the easy means, so that we don't have to gamble on lifetimes of arduous struggle in the hope of fully awakening it.

Improved Mental State

Once this dormant witnessing awareness is fully awakened in us, with the right leadership and practical, effective methods, we can *nurture* this spiritual awareness, over time causing it to blossom into a *paradise of Joy, Inspiration and Well-Being.* I was Blessed by my Gurudev in this way with the one missing element that is the difference that makes the difference – **Grace!**

So, what is this Grace I speak of? Grace is the Power, the Love that rescues us from the entanglement of worldliness and, like a boat, carries us across the illusion of this world to that distant shore of Joy, Peace, and the Bliss of The Absolute. Grace is That which frees us from the bondage of ignorance that keeps God concealed from us. *This Grace comes from a Master.*

My Shri Gurudev has said, "For the sake of Joy, a person does all kinds of things, not knowing that happiness lies within. Such a person is like the musk deer that carries the precious fragrance of musk in its own navel. But out of ignorance, the musk deer keeps searching for that fragrance outside. The breeze carries the fragrance of the musk toward the mountains, and the deer runs eagerly in that direction.

It runs and runs searching for that fragrance and eventually dies. Then the people who live in the mountains cut open the deer and remove the musk. It is the same story with a human being. In spite of everything one does, a person does not see lasting happiness. But if, by good fortune, he/she meets a Saint, a great being, then a person can become completely happy." Here, my Gurudev is describing my poor condition before meeting Him – a condition that so many of you also share.

It is said that the mind loves the places it frequents the most and then, as a result, we become what we obey. An improved mental state is one in which the mind has been trained to turn within on a regular, consistent basis. In this way, the mind becomes what it meditates on.

So, our mental state vastly improves when the tired, restless mind is made to turn within long enough to desire the company of the Self - the company of that Shakti power that brings the experience of Bliss, Happiness, Fearlessness and Content. Such a mind becomes like gold, withstanding the test of time with great fortitude of Peace and Joy. This leads to a mental state that is awash in the Bliss, Inspiration and Intuition of the Ultimate Reality and Cause – God.

With the daily spiritual practice and leadership in the methods for changing lifetimes of useless understandings and false notions, your mental state improves to the point where the mind becomes sharper, full of mental clarity and the most useful vision for attaining the highest experience of what living is. Such an improved mental state naturally leads to release from the prison of useless emotions.

Emotional Resilience

Are you enjoying your emotions or are they enjoying you? If you contemplate this, even for a short while, you will begin to discard the tired, worn out noise intended to suggest that connectedness to each other is based on 'emotional availability.'

Although there is great usefulness in empathy, there is no usefulness in enabling worthless causes like enjoying mutual enslavement in emotional reactions. And *Love* is what connects us, *not* the expression of what appears to be mutually shared emotions. *Love is Love, precisely because it makes no distinctions and is unconditional, thereby rendering Freedom to the true expression of Humanity.* And we love each other best by seeing God in each other.

Therefore, *Emotional Resilience is freedom* – the freedom to express one's Humanity *fully* without becoming a slave to the emotions. Here, in Nityananda Shaktipat Yoga, you are taught proved methods for developing emotional resilience in a way that gives the experience of inner Joy, regardless of what kind of emotion is being expressed, and regardless of the degree of intensity of expression.

In other words, your inner state is never swayed away from that of Peace and Bliss, regardless of how your Humanity is being expressed in the moment. You come to know that *the act* of expression is not who you are, but rather a tool that you engage.

Vibrant Health

Spirituality and the journey to Joy that comprises retracing one's steps back to God, does not exclude the quality of life embodied in vibrant health. Here we make one very important distinction connected to the first of the 4 pillars, The Spiritual Power.

The physical body is the child of the mind. And the mind is the child of the Self – God. We embrace this understanding to ensure that we don't get carried away by our senses and emotions through attachment, attraction and aversion, each of which are a play of the Gunas and the Malas - the inner impurities for which the Shaktipat Kriya Process is the cure. Still, we want to be in a healthy vehicle in the body, at least long enough to realize the goal of our existence here, with a comfortable quality of life.

Therefore, we begin applying lifestyle medicine for vibrant health of the physical body, with the understanding that *the body is the temple in which God resides*. Because the Ultimate Reality, the Indweller, resides in the form we call 'body,' we respect and care for the physical body with this intention. This is the only way to truly respect the gift God has granted us in the miraculous nest that is the physical body.

So, our intention for vibrant health is to dwell in a pure, clean and healthy temple, in order to maintain the vehicle that allows us to engage our existence here, free of the distraction of illness and disease, whenever possible, given one's Karmas.

Freedom from this kind of distraction paves the way for endurance in realizing the purpose of a human birth – to retrace one's steps back to God – without attachment to what is fleeting and ephemeral. It is with this understanding and intention that we also offer programs in holistic nutrition, vibrational healing and holistic lifestyle medicine.

These 4 pillars combined, form an indestructible foundation for nurturing the receipt of Shaktipat and the realization of the goal of the Shaktipat Kriya Process, also known as Sadhana. They are offered for this purpose alone.

Chapter 2
My Experiences
Before and After Shaktipat

My Life and Early Career
In The Performing Arts

My mother was a great opera diva who performed all over the world. She had a great career that was cut short when she decided to raise my brother and me. One might say that she decided to express herself through us. My mother trained us in the Performing Arts. She taught us to sing, dance and act.

As a result, I had an early career as a child actor in starring roles on Broadway, landing my earliest roles in the musical *Maggie Flynn* and the play *The Great White Hope*. My younger years were spent travelling as a working actor with many known celebrities of the time. I enjoyed this period of my life because I had the opportunity to make audiences contemplate, laugh and cry by performing in shows and I loved interacting with people.

I left my acting career in my late teens to pursue music. I studied violin, piano, composition and conducting, graduating from Manhattan School of Music with a degree in performance. Right out of school, I spent several years earning my living exclusively as a performing artist. During this time, I saw the powerful effect the Performing Arts have on people's inner state.

I saw that a skilled performing artist has the power to take people anywhere they want to go, to experience any emotion and any state of being, at least temporarily. It was at this time that I decided to compose music and learn music improvisation as a means of experiencing my creativity and becoming more creative. This experience of creating changed my vision of the world. It was my first real glimpse into the mystery of all creation, something I wanted to know much more about.

Holistic Healing

In my early teens, I suffered a variety of illnesses, one right after the other. My mother became very concerned about my health and felt I needed a change in diet. She bought me a book and demanded I read it. That book was *Sugar Blues*, a popular book by Gloria Swanson and Bill Dufty that spoke of the dangers of processed sugar and processed foods and outlined a movement that was fast-growing in America at the time, *Macrobiotics*.

I became invigorated by the concept that a diet high in organic veggies, legumes, whole grains and fruit could change awareness. So, I engaged in the study of Macrobiotics, changing my diet completely by starting with a 3-week, brown rice fast. I stopped eating red meat, chicken and pork. I removed white sugar from my diet and I stopped smoking. My health did improve drastically. As a result, I moved into the Kushi Institute, run by Michio Kushi, one of the founders of the Macrobiotic movement here in the West. There I studied Oriental Medicine, Macrobiotics, and learned to cook.

Michio's philosophy was that one can experience a closeness to the Self and a desire to know the Self by eating a diet that aligns one's body with its natural vibration. This includes eating foods grown in season, in the region one lives in. In my case, it worked. Similar to the experience I had when becoming more creative in the Performing Arts, Macrobiotics and my time spent in the company of Michio Kushi studying Oriental Medicine and graduating from the Kushi Institute did alter my vision of the world and my perception of life. My longing to become more spiritual increased as a result.

Experience of Death

In junior high school I became obsessed with all things occult. I consumed books on white and black witchcraft before finally settling on the Tarot. I actually became quite knowledgeable and had a steady clientele of fellow classmates (and their parents) who came to our house for readings. The Tarot opened me to the understanding that other worlds exist and power is not simply that which is defined by money and political influence.

During these years, I developed a psychic ability I did not know I had. I would often see visions or get premonitions about people just before they arrived for a Tarot reading. I then shared with them what I saw without reading the cards. This started to happen more and more regularly. Again, all this served to intensify my desire to know God.

During my career in the Performing Arts, I had spent a good deal of time getting to know the celebrities I performed with. Later, while pursuing business ownership, I was mentored by wealthy business owners who were millionaires. I came to know them personally and also spent time with their families.

What I observed in these people is that, even though they had fulfilled so many of their worldly desires and fantasies, they weren't happy. They did not know peace. When I asked them "What is Love?" they did not have an answer. When I asked, "Are you happy?," they answered "Who is really happy? I'm normal."

Through this experience I decided that the people whose lifestyles I wanted, the people who I had looked up to and wanted to be like for so long, had not attained what I was seeking. So, I decided not to pursue their lifestyles.

It was at this time that I started to ask the questions: **Is this all there is? What is fate? What is destiny? Who am I? Why am I here? Why was I born?**

During this period of my life I had an experience of death. I was riding in a car with my mother and brother. The car suddenly veered off the road on a sharp corner and flipped over into a ravine. The car landed upside down and was almost completely flattened. My mother and brother were thrown several feet from the car and escaped injury. I was pinned inside the car. A boulder had smashed through the roof of the car and landed on my chest. My body was pinned between this boulder and the floor. I was unable to breathe.

I was not breathing but I was still conscious. Suddenly, my awareness left my body and I found myself hovering several feet in the air above the wreck. I could see my mother and brother on the road being tended to by paramedics. As I looked straight down, I saw my body trapped inside the car and I saw rescue workers with saws, carving away the metal in an attempt to get to me. *I hovered in the air watching this scene with complete calm for several minutes.*

I then heard my mother screaming my name hysterically. With this, I found myself back in my body. I was being dragged from the wreck and my breathing began again on its own. As the rescue workers attempted to revive me, I sat up on my own and called out to my mother and brother. Although my chest was a little bruised, I had no other injuries.

This experience caused me to pause and contemplate my entire life. I knew I had experienced death. *I wanted to know who it was that was able to witness my body and this entire event in this way.* This was the first time that I understood that there is more to a human being than just this body.

My Years As A Seeker

I first started meditating as part of my study of martial arts. I studied Karate, Kung Fu and Jeet Kun Do. Each of these disciplines required the study and practice of Meditation. The Meditation was of the Buddhist tradition and, as a result, I embarked upon the study of Zen Buddhism for several years.

Although Zen Buddhism sparked my interest in Meditation, I felt there was still something missing. My mind still troubled me and I was not able to quiet it. After Buddhism, I engaged in several different meditation paths, including Transcendental Meditation. I followed a number of gurus during this time, all of whom were great teachers in their own right.

Still, I did not experience the bliss of Meditation that I had heard about. I found it difficult to enter into a thought-free state, let alone maintain it. I later realized that what was missing for me was the spiritual awakening that would allow me to experience a more spontaneous Meditation. I also needed a master teacher who had completely realized the goal of his own practice.

I had become very wary of cults and gurus and I had become skeptical of spiritual paths in general. But still, deep in my heart, I knew I needed the right Guru and approach. I had yet to find such a path.

My Upbringing In Churches

I was born a Catholic and raised a Catholic in my early youth. As a young boy, I went to Catholic school and became an altar boy in my local church. I embraced Catholicism completely at that time, mostly because I loved the stories of Jesus Christ and his life. I had always wished that I could have lived in a time when such a being existed in the flesh. My mother, however, was raised in the Baptist tradition. After my mother and father divorced, I spent a great deal of time in the Baptist church.

I loved the ritual of the Catholic ceremony and I really took to the Gospel tradition of the Baptists. "Catching the spirit" also intrigued me. Although I loved aspects of both these traditions, I wanted to know and wanted to have a direct experience of God, as a constant in my life. I did not feel I was getting that from either of these paths.

The experience of joy, peace, bliss, happiness, abundance, fearlessness, courage and strength - these are things that I wanted to stop talking about over cocktails and coffee and wanted to experience directly, not just a little or once in a while, but on a *constant* basis.

Starting in my late teens, I came to observe that, here in the West, many religious paths form a type of "spectator" practice where intellectual discourses are dispensed and then the celebration is over before it even gets started - *like someone talking about a fabulous meal without ever serving it up*. It was this experience, and the lack of teachers who practiced fully what they preached, that led me away from the traditional approach to religion and spirituality that I found to be so common.

I had to find something that *was not* just about the psychology of religion, but something that would give me a direct experience of the Ultimate Reality.

Shaktipat – Full Kundalini Awakening

There is no point in continuing to remain a seeker. **In fact, the point of all spiritual seeking is to find a way to *end your seeking*.** *To bring your seeking to an end, full Shakti Awakening and the leadership of a living Siddha Guru is necessary.* Such Beings are rare.

God is always watching. God is always listening. It's important to remember this. Crossing paths with a Shakipat Guru is something *we* cause to happen. The spiritually-perfected companion in the Living Master does not seek us out. We make a request and God grants that request in our crossing paths with a Siddha Guru. Some people remember exactly when they made the request in the present life or a previous life, others have forgotten. But the request was made, nonetheless.

For me, the request began with those questions I shared that I had during my early seeking: **Is this all there is? What is fate? What is destiny? Who am I? Why am I here? Why was I born?** Then I made a direct request to fully know the answers to these questions. That request is what caused me to cross paths with the catalyst for realizing my true nature, my spiritual Guru. I caused the meeting with the Sadguru (as we all do). This decision to seek out a live path and to be led by a Self-realized Love being was reinforced by two visions I had in my senior year at Manhattan School of Music.

My Visions of Jesus Christ

At that time, I still considered myself to be a Christian. Even though I had stopped attending church services, I worshipped Jesus Christ at home in my own way. I was studying Religion and Philosophy with V. Saly Ph.D., a renowned Czech philosopher and teacher who was in residence at Manhattan School of Music at that time. Dr. Saly used to give discourses in the lobby and cafeteria of the school.

Very often he spoke about the saints of other traditions and the mystics of Eastern civilization. Dr. Saly also did dream interpretation and was very popular among the students for this reason. The first vision was quite incredible and reinforced in me the understanding that my worship of Jesus Christ had borne fruit in the form of direct guidance from him.

I had taken a great interest in the research that was going on at that time into the *Holy Shroud of Turin*, reputed to be the cloth that Christ's body was wrapped in when he was taken down off the cross and entombed. I had been corresponding with the two American scientists who were part of the team that was analyzing the shroud to determine its authenticity.

One morning I woke from an intense vision. *Jesus Christ appeared to me and told me this:* "You cannot go any further without a living master. I am sending you to your Master. With my blessing he comes to you. Embrace him with all your heart and know that the Master is the path."

When I awoke from this vision I found a set of outstretched hands on the wall of my apartment. These hands looked as if they had been painted on the wall. My live-in girlfriend, a devout Christian, got out of the bed and sat beside me, letting out a scream. She then told me that the hands were those of Jesus Christ.

As if to prove her point, she proceeded to pull a picture of Christ from her purse which showed him with his hands outstretched in exactly the same fashion. We spent the better part of the day proving that the hands were really there by trying to scrape and clean them off the wall. After a while, it became obvious the only way they were coming off was if we repainted.

That evening, as I fell asleep, I had another vision. I was standing on a plateau, very high up, overlooking a huge riverbed. The river was dry. As I looked off into the distance, I saw thousands of people attempting to get across this massive riverbed. When I looked down at the riverbed again, I saw the bodies and heads of lambs everywhere. There was also blood in the riverbed. As the people drew closer to me, I started lifting them up on to the plateau I was standing on. There was another being who I did not recognize at the time, standing next to me, instructing me and helping me to lift them up.

I woke up from this dream in a trance-like state and I was not able to go back to sleep for the rest of the night. The next morning, I called Dr. Saly and scheduled a time to see him. I shared these two visions with him. His response was that I had reached a level in my spiritual growth that I would not be able to go beyond without a living spiritual master!

He told me that the experience of God I longed for would only come through spending time in the company of a Saint or lineage of holy beings. When I told him that I didn't know any Saints, Dr. Saly reinforced what I heard in the dreams: that I would, somehow, find this; that I would not have to go searching for this, but would be led right to the door. He then told me to remain aware and watch for a sign.

My Turning Point

I was 22 years old at the time. It was a hot summer for Vermont, great for swimming in the local swimming hole, something I did a lot of when I went to Vermont. My violin teacher, Carroll Glen, and her husband, pianist Eugene List, ran a small, lively classical music festival in southern Vermont. I had just graduated from Manhattan School of Music and this was to be my last year performing at this festival.

Back in Manhattan my "on again off again" girlfriend was minding our apartment. We had gone to school together and we were still living together. Our relationship was coming to an end and the summer afforded the two of us an opportunity to be separate long enough to let that decision set in.

In the midst of withdrawing from my 4-year relationship with my live-in mate, I fell in love with another woman who was performing at the festival. This woman finally told me she had a live-in boyfriend of her own back in Iceland who was coming to visit her at the festival. Unbeknownst to me, my live-in girlfriend had a "mole" at the festival who had reported my newfound romance to her. So, even though we were breaking up, my almost-to-be ex-girlfriend got on a bus and headed to the festival to see what this woman looked like for herself.

Now the ending to this story is somewhat of a paradox. I wound up losing both women simultaneously. And, for several months after the festival, *I battled with depression and a profound sense of loss that seemed, at the same time, illogical and outright ridiculous!* Yet, I couldn't shake it. I wouldn't shake it. I was really attached to this pain, this gloating over losing women and finding women and losing them again.

On top of that, after three years of making my living doing nothing but performing as a soloist and ensemble player, each of the programs that employed me announced they might be folding due to government budget cuts. So, I suddenly found myself putting down my violin and picking up the local help wanted ads.

I was so depressed that I found myself, for the second time in my life, contemplating my own existence. Then those questions came up again: the same ones I had asked myself before. *Is this all there is? What is fate? What is destiny? Who am I? Why am I here? Why was I born?*

Amazing Grace, how sweet the sound
That saved a wretch like me
I once was lost but now I'm found
Blind but now I see

Shaktipat – My Full Kundalini Awakening

These questions were soon answered. After attending an introductory event in Manhattan, I purchased Muktananda Paramahamsa's autobiography, *Play of Consciousness.* One winter evening I decided to begin reading it. I will never forget this glorious evening. It was February 23, 1979, two days before my birthday. It was the greatest and most precious gift of my life!

As I opened the book, I kept closing it to gaze on Muktananda's picture on the front cover. I was unable to begin reading because I kept going back to that picture. It was so alive! It was at this moment that I received Shaktipat from that picture of Muktananda Baba! Some of the *initial* experiences I had upon this full Kundalini Awakening were:

- Immediate increase in body temperature. I felt like my body was on fire.
- A decrease in body temperature. I felt that my body had gone completely cold.
- Spontaneous Hatha Yoga postures with complete flexibility. I had never studied Hatha Yoga before.
- Intense flashes of light inside: blue, gold, white, red, black. These were phenomenal.

- Huge and quick emotional swings. These were not triggered by any interaction and came up spontaneously.
- Loss of body consciousness in Meditation.
- Hearing mantras welling up inside me, spontaneously.
- Visions of Saints not known to me at the time. Later I found out that these are Saints in our Shiva lineage.

After having these experiences, immediately I wrote to Baba with my questions and to determine the next step. He was on tour in the U.S. at the time and I wanted immediate instruction for my Sadhana, until I was able to join the tour. I received that instruction and was placed in the loving care of Swamis living in the Manhattan ashram. Shortly after that, I took Baba as my Guru and surrendered to his direct and loving leadership a short while later. What a glorious time that was!

This all led to my receipt of Shaktipat again from Muktananda Paramahamsa in several weekend intensives he led that I later participated in. In the first intensive, I found myself in a room of more than two-thousand people. During the first meditation session, Baba walked through rows of people, touching them in various places. When he got to me, I felt his hand on the top of my head. He then pressed a point at the top of my forehead, and also one between my eyebrows. Immediately, there was an explosion in my head and what I perceived to be a very intelligent force began moving down my spine.

At the same time, there was another explosion at the base of my spine. A subtle energy proceeded to move up my spine. These two forces, one dripping down from my vibrating head and the other moving up from my spine, collided in my heart center. There was another explosion. Immediately, I was awash with waves and waves of Love like I had never known. I came out of that meditation crying tears of Joy, feeling like I had come home. And those waves of Love and tears of Joy continued over the next several days before beginning to subside.

This combination of events, along with Muktananda's leadership and instruction, established me in my Sadhana. The experiences I share in this book are all due to this awakening and the loving leadership, tests and training I received during the Shakipat Kriya Process, my Sadhana.

As I engaged in the Shaktipat Kriya process, I had many more transformative experiences, some of which I share in this book. I also requested and was accepted as a disciple in this Shaktipat lineage, and my life was filled with the *Bliss* of the inner Self. *For that, I am forever grateful.*

Chapter 3
Authentic Shaktipat
and Who Can Give It

One must seek the shortest route and fastest means to
get back home, to turn one's inner spark into a blaze and then
to merge and identify with that greater fire which ignited the
spark.
~ Bhagawan Nityananda of Ganeshpuri

Shaktipat is the Grace of an entire lineage of
Siddha Gurus. It is said that God is always favorably
disposed to his devotees. This must certainly go
double for me. It is almost unfathomable that my
Lord has chosen to work through me in this way.
Why would He choose a wretch like me? It could
only be due to my Guru's Grace. So, I still always
remember the Grace of my Guru, the Grace of
Bhagawan Nityananda and our entire lineage.
It is only when our lineage is pleased that the Grace-
bestowing power of the Self can flow through Kedarji
in a way that is understood and experienced by those
people who have Bhakti, *Longing*. So, I ask you to
keep an open mind and heart as you read on.

The purpose of *full Shakti Awakening*, also
referred to as *Shaktipat* or *Kundalini Awakening*, is to
set the foundation for the destruction of conditioning
created by samskaras, the karmic impressions,
leanings and tendencies of so many past lives and the
present life. Full Kundalini Awakening begins a
spontaneous process of the purification of lifetimes
of karmas. We refer to this purification as the
Shaktipat Kriya Process or *Sadhana*.

This is an approach that gradually allows us to
live in a state of Grace. It is called the easy or
spontaneous means because lifetimes of ardent

struggle and practice utilizing many different spiritual techniques is replaced with this initiation given by a Shaktipat Guru, making the practice necessary for going beyond the mind and beyond the senses, spontaneous and free-flowing.

In our approach, a Shaktipat Guru who is a Sadguru (true spiritual leader), is a being who has stored up the maximum amount of Divine Conscious Energy (Shakti) necessary to fully awaken this dormant energy in others. Such a being is one who is also a master in guiding the fully awakened Shakti to full expansion, an experience in which the spiritual aspirant rests in the uninterrupted state of *Pure Perceiving Awareness* that brings the exalted experience of *the fullness of Humanity in the constant delight of the inner Self.*

This is a matter of true spiritual leadership. This Grace-bestowing power is transmitted by the Siddha Guru to awaken Kundalini (dormant spiritual energy), and to revolutionize one's meditation practice and spiritual life. Those who have had a lapse in their spiritual practice, or feel the need for additional support, also return to the Shaktipat Guru to receive this transmission of Grace-bestowing power.

This awakening is the transmission of energy that makes meditation more spontaneous while invoking the inner healing process that purifies the heart and allows one to embrace a spiritual lifestyle of Joy and Content. Shaktipat deepens and accelerates our spiritual practice in this way.

After this awakening is received, a purification process begins whereby, over time and with regular spiritual practice, the Shakti pierces and purifies all of the subtle energy centers within the physical and subtle bodies.

Over time, this awakening leads to a person becoming completely established in his/her own Joy,

with the constant awareness and experience of the
Ultimate Reality inside and everywhere. By the
nurturing of this full Shakti awakening through daily
spiritual practice, we experience an inner unfolding of
awareness that leads to states of higher and higher
spiritual, witnessing awareness. Gradually we secure
the Bliss, Joy, Peace, Happiness, and Content that is
our birthright. *In our school, we have documented this
transformation in others over a period of many years.*

All that I have, my spiritual attainment of the
Self, is due to the descent of Grace bestowed upon
me by my Guru, through *Shaktipat*. I could not have
realized my identity with the Self without this spiritual
awakening. I am sharing from my personal
experience. For an even better understanding of the
mystical experience of Shaktipat, you can read
Devatma Shakti by Swami Vishnu Tirtha, or *A Guide to
Shaktipat* by Swami Shivom Tirth, Vishnu Tirtha's
successor. In addition, the following Shastras and
Agamas also contain accounts of the experience of
Shaktipat, the Grace of a Siddha Guru and the
workings of Kundalini Shakti: *Mahayoga Vijnana,
Yogavani, Shiva Sutras, Pratyabhijnahridayam, Tantraloka,
Shivadrishti, Jnaneshwari, Kularnava Tantra.*

Shaktipat is the beginning, the middle and the
end. In the company of a spiritual leader in the living
Shaktipat Guru, the experience of Shaktipat continues
to unfold on many levels. So, with the instruction and
leadership of the living Shaktipat Guru, Shaktipat
becomes the ongoing experience of Guru's Grace. It
should be treated with the highest reverence. *Indeed, it
is the miracle of Grace.*

The approach to attaining the Freedom of the
constant delight in the Self, by means of the
awakened inner spiritual energy, is known as the Yoga
of the Siddhas that, in our school, we also refer to as
Nityananda Shaktipat Yoga. Ours is a time-honored,
proven Yoga Science based in the bond of power of a

very long, unbroken lineage of Shaktipat Gurus that dates back to the pre-Bronze Age. It is named *Nityananda*, which means the eternal Bliss of the Absolute, after Bhagawan Nityananda of Ganeshpuri, a highly revered sage of our lineage.

Experience of Indescribable Joy In Daily Mundane Life

One of the biggest complaints among seekers and yogis who have experienced some type of initiation is that they begin to have good meditations when sitting in asana with their eyes closed, *but they don't experience the joy and peace of their meditation when going about their daily mundane activities.* They feel great in meditation but, once they are up and about, it's life as usual without any lasting change in their experience of the mundane world or the people around them.

For this reason, there is a specific approach to giving full Shakti Awakening that is engaged by the Siddha Gurus of our lineage. It is based on the principles and techniques set forth in the Shaivism of The Spanda School of Vasuguptacharya and Abhinavaguptacharya (not the Shaivism as defined by Google or Wikipedia). This is Shaktipat by and into the highest or purest vibration of Divine Consciousness.

Through this type of initiation, a seeker begins to experience God's two aspects, the immanent and the transcendental, reverberating in one's being *as one Divine force.* This initiation also sets in motion a process wherein the seeker begins to experience all the stages or levels of Manifestation (tattvas) within one's own being, from Earth up to the absolute Paramashiva (the one, formless Supreme Principle). The Chakras (spiritual centers) above the head are also opened.

For this reason, we say that this is full Shakti awakening. It allows you to begin experiencing God in everything and everyone, everywhere. This Shaktipat is the basis for the ongoing experience of Meditation as you go about the mundane activities of your life.

The awakening of Kundalini Shakti within a seeker first destroys *Anava mala.* Anava mala (in this reference, mala means taint or impurity) is what causes the feeling of imperfection and the feeling or notion of being separate from God. This mala gives rise to all of the other imperfections and limitations experienced by a living being. Shaktipat is first necessary in order to remove Anava mala. This mala cannot be removed in any other way.

After this full Shakti Awakening is received, a purification process begins whereby, over time and with regular Meditation and other spiritual practices, Kundalini pierces and purifies all of the subtle energy centers within the physical and subtle body (the subtle body houses the ego idea, the individual intellect and all of the psychic instruments). In the physical presence of the Shaktipat Guru, this initiation becomes an expansive experience of that Master's Grace that is "stepped-up" or quickened through the Shaktipat Kriya Process.

It is within the subtle body (Sushumna) that all of the impressions (vasanas) from past lives and the present life are stored. These impressions give rise to our emotional states, our fears, our memories, our tendencies, habits and leanings, etc. These represent our Karmas.

After the receipt of Shaktipat, with the nurturing provided by daily Meditation, Chanting and other spiritual practices, and the direct leadership offered by the Sadguru, these impressions are removed by the rising Kundalini Shakti, freeing the

aspirant of duality and the false notion that one is just
a person, just the body, mind and senses.

Upon receiving Shaktipat, one should nurture
this Divine Energy of Consciousness through
Meditation, Chanting, Prayer, Contemplation and
Selfless Service, so that the Shakti may rise through
the Sushumna and all the subtle energy points,
purifying everything in its path. As this occurs, the
devotee's understanding becomes ripe with the
knowledge that this Shiva-Shakti power is the Guru.

Over time, this process leads to a person
becoming completely established in his/her own
Bliss, with the constant awareness and experience of
the Self, the Ultimate Reality and Cause, inside and
everywhere. Over time, and with practice, all past
impressions and karmas are burned in the purifying
fire of this transformative Grace, the Kriya Shakti of
the living Siddha Guru. Through the nurturing of full
Shakti Awakening by daily spiritual practice, the
student experiences an inner unfolding of awareness
that leads to increasing states of higher and pure
spiritual witnessing awareness.

This purification leads to the *Natural, Free
State of Being* from which one worships the Shiva-
Shakti power by becoming that power, *by becoming what
one already is.* It is a state of incomparable Bliss and
Contentment, the state of ultimate true knowledge.
This Shiva-Shakti power is the energy substratum of
everything. Therefore, it is the highest power. The
fact is we all need a power source in order to evoke
any type of transformation that is sustainable.

What About Spontaneous Awakenings?

There is a lot of talk today on the Internet and
elsewhere, regarding 'spontaneous awakenings' of
Kundalini. This is an apparent attempt, on the part of
teachers who have not served a Shaktipat Guru or

been authorized by such a being to give Shaktipat, to promote the notion that one does not need an authentic Shaktipat Guru to experience Shaktipat.

And, upon closer examination of what people are stating was a spontaneous awakening of Kundalini, it becomes clear that people are calling any energetic experience Shaktipat. In fact, many of these people have experienced being healed of a particular condition or have experienced a movement of energy similar to Reiki healing or Qi Gong energetics. Although beneficial in other ways, these are not connected to Shaktipat.

Is it possible to have a spontaneous, full Kundalini Awakening? From scientific discoveries, we know that entire galaxies can spontaneously disappear into a black hole. From the same discoveries we know that this is a *very rare event*. Can the Sun stop giving light and disappear from the sky? Yes. We know this because there was an ice age on this planet. However, we also know that this is a *very rare phenomenon*, not having re-occurred in our existence here for millennia.

Spontaneous, full kundalini awakenings *are even more rare than these phenomenon*. Then there is what needs to take place after the full Kundalini awakening, in order to fully nurture and protect the rising Kundalini. So, just as only a trained doctor or other very qualified practitioner can properly diagnose an illness, based on years of experience, evidence-based research and testing, only a Shaktipat Guru who is a Sadguru can lead you in understanding and experiencing what Shaktipat really is.

The Noise

The Internet has become THE resource that people go to for the information they rely on for making decisions of all kinds. This is both useful and useless at the same time. Since I'm certain you are aware of the useful part, let me address the useless part in the context of why Shaktipat is essential for permanent spiritual transformation.

The Internet and social media provide an inexpensive and effective means for anyone you don't know personally to position themselves as experts in a given field. In some cases, they *are* the top experts in their field. But, in so many cases, they are not. That's the useless part. Online marketing experts call this phenomenon *The Noise*.

Indeed, there are many available, powerful, Internet business development tools (one of them being AI) that allow inexperienced novices to position themselves as experts. Consequently, so many people you don't know personally are using that fact to convince you, on a web page or in social media, that they are the 'go to' for what you are looking for. These advanced, Internet business development tools make this easy to do. Many more people than you can even count are doing it. This is no less the case than in the context of Shaktipat.

Who Can Give Shaktipat?

Authentic Shaktipat Gurus are very rare. When this highest and greatest transmission of God's Grace bestowing power is transmitted by a genuine Shaktipat Guru who is in a lineage of such beings, the effect is miraculous.

Therefore, an authentic Shaktipat Guru is one who is in an *unbroken lineage* of Shaktipat Gurus and has served as a Disciple of another Shaktipat Sadguru in a lineage of such beings. The following applies:

- Authorized by his/her Guru to transmit the Grace-bestowing power of Shaktipat.

- Stored up the maximum amount of this Grace-bestowing power over a period of years of performing Sadhana under the direct leadership of another Shaktipat Sadguru in a lineage of such beings.
- Served his/her Guru for a period of *years*. This is not a being who attended a weekend seminar or a few days of courses with a known Sadguru. An authentic Shaktipat Guru is a being who has been *molded by his/her Sadguru.*

Origins of Shaktipat
For Full Kundalini Awakening

The experience and knowledge of what authentic Shaktipat is was brought to the West and Europe by Siddha Gurus - perfected Self-realized Love Beings. Equally important, these masters were in a lineage of authentic Shaktipat Gurus. Such Siddha Gurus served their own Masters for many years. In this way, they earned their Guru's Grace. Most of all, this is how they attained the authority and power to transmit this most precious Grace-bestowing power of God. This profound Blessing was not known outside of the East before these beings traveled outside of their regions!

There are people who have the ability to transmit energy or an energetic experience to you. However, this ability alone does not automatically qualify them to transmit this Grace-bestowing power. In fact, a person who has attained a healing certification, for example, or a Reiki master certification, etc. is not, automatically, qualified to give Shaktipat. And yet, many such people are claiming to do so.

There is nothing wrong with people following what they believe to be their calling, where meditation, yoga, spiritual teaching, healing, etc. are concerned. *We wish these people well in their endeavors.* However, in Nityananda Shaktipat Yoga, it is our feeling that such people should be more honest about their attainment and lack of authority.

It's Just Business, Unfortunately

Remember my discussion about The Noise (see above)? In many cases, people who have never received Shaktipat are making claims about it. Additionally, there are even spiritual teachers who claim to give it, never having received it and never having served another Shaktipat Guru.

Why? It's just business, unfortunately. To maintain viability of any offering using the Internet as the primary marketing tool, people have to build their platform. This begins with creating compelling content that gets people to give their email address and become active email openers and social media participants. Some people using this tool want to serve the public's greater good first and have the expertise and authority (by way of experience) to do so. Others are only interested in collecting followers to increase income and notoriety. Some want both. *Seekers beware.*

Does a person needing heart surgery go to a doctor who has never performed the surgery, or to a surgeon who has done so successfully many times, by way of mentoring under another expert? Does a person needing expert legal representation in a court of law hire a paralegal or a seasoned, litigating attorney? So, use your head in your search for authentic Shaktipat, as you do in other matters of life.

Seeker Beware! 13 Questions You Should Ask Before Receiving Shaktipat and The 5 Common Mistakes You Should Avoid.

People who have never received authentic Shaktipat from a Shaktipat Sadguru in a lineage of such beings are in no position to talk about what Shaktipat is. Further, someone who has not been led by a Sadguru who was led in the same way, in the gradual unfolding of the fully awakened Kundalini is in no position to give Shaktipat or tell you what it is.

There are those who say that the receipt of Shaktipat from a Shaktipat Sadguru is unnecessary to awaken Kundalini. Additionally, most of these same people admit that they have never received Shaktipat from a Shaktipat Guru. If they've never received authentic Shaktipat, they have nothing on which to make a comparison between the two! Therefore, such statements are mere opinion and do not represent the truth. For all these reasons, I share the following with you.

13 QUESTIONS TO ASK *BEFORE* YOU CONSIDER RECEIVING SHAKTIPAT FROM ANYONE

1. Who is your Guru?
2. How long did you serve your Guru (or) how long have you served your Guru?
3. How much time did you or do you spend in the company of your Guru each month?
4. What is your feeling for your Guru?
5. Were you accepted as a Disciple of your Guru?
6. Did your Guru have a Guru who he/she served for an extended period of time as a Disciple?
7. How did your Guru receive the authorization to give Shaktipat?

8. How did you receive the authorization to give Shaktipat and when were you authorized?

9. Do you have any written documentation or something other than a picture that shows that you had/have a Guru and that you served that Guru for an extended period of time?

10. Or are there other people who also served your Guru in the period that you did, who can verify that you did so?

11. Do you have video testimonials at your web site from people who have received Shaktipat from you?

12. Are some of those people available to speak to me directly about their experience?

13. After giving Shaktipat, what support do you provide in the form of programs, course of study and leadership to nurture the unfolding of the awakened Kundalini?

(These questions are answered for Kedarji at the end of this book.)

Do You Make These 5 Common Mistakes When Seeking A Shaktipat Sadguru? - Avoid Them.

1. Talk is just that, talk. In so many cases people claiming to be spiritual teachers or leaders are *only* very good communicators. To be a good communicator is necessary. But don't make your decision to receive Shaktipat from anyone based on that person's ability to communicate or entertain alone. Spend some time studying that being's written works and video content. Also, unless you live at a great distance from that being, visit his/her ashram or center, attend some programs and spend some time in the physical company of that being before deciding. Otherwise, dig down into the video content and blogging provided and read some of that person's books, to start.

2. My Shri Gurudev used to say that the false Guru market has gotten so large because the number of false disciples has increased exponentially. Shaktipat Sadgurus are true spiritual leaders who have become the principles and practices they instruct others in. They are pure beings who live in a state of constant delight. If you look for common personality traits in the Guru that are shared by you, your friends/family and popular culture, if you look for mundane desires in the Guru that you are fond of pursuing, you'll certainly get the wrong Guru.

We go to a Siddha Guru and we seek to receive initiation from such a Guru to imbibe qualities, habits, tendencies and spiritual principles of great power and purity, that we have not yet attained or not yet fully attained. Look for these in the one you are seeking to receive Shaktipat from.

3. Research the Guru's lineage before receiving Shaktipat from such a being. Authentic Shaktipat Gurus are very rare. This is because their ability to transmit the Grace-bestowing power of God in a way that fully awakens your Kundalini *safely* comes from the power of the lineage of Shaktipat Gurus they are in. So, lineage is very important when choosing a Shaktipat Guru.

4. If you receive Shaktipat from an authentic Shaktipat Guru, after initiation, spend some time testing that Guru before entering into the Shaktipat Kriya Process of Sadhana (tutelage under the living Master). This should be done so that you are certain that you are with the right one, before you make the choice to be led in the journey of nurturing the awakened Kundalini over an extended period of time. *This nurturing for the unfolding of Kundalini is imperative* and requires obeying instruction given by the living Guru.

So, test first. The way in which to test the Guru is spoken about at length later in this book.

5. Take your time. If you decide to follow, take your time in performing the test of the Guru. Typically, people do so over a period of 6-24 months of spending time in direct physical proximity to the Guru. In other words, test by keeping the Guru's company and testing the Guru's instruction in the laboratory of your own existence.

Now, let's take a closer look at what authentic Shaktipat is and the journey of unfolding after its receipt.

Shaktipat - The Easy Means

I took a permanent, quantum leap in my spiritual and well-being transformation, with just one touch! This quantum leap embodied in the Shaktipat Blessing is called *the easy or spontaneous means*. It is so called because lifetimes of arduous struggle and practice utilizing many different spiritual techniques is replaced with this initiation given by a Shaktipat Guru. This makes the practice necessary for going beyond the mind and beyond the senses spontaneous and free flowing.

A Shaktipat Guru who is a Sadguru (true Guru), is a being who has stored up the maximum amount of Divine Conscious Energy (Shakti) necessary to fully awaken this dormant spiritual awareness in others, *without ever depleting his/her maximum store of Shakti.* **Such a being is also a Master at *leading* devotees in such a way that the fully awakened Shakti is properly nurtured to *full expansion.***

This is an experience in which the spiritual aspirant eventually rests in the uninterrupted state of

Pure Perceiving Awareness that brings the exalted experience of *the fullness of Humanity in the constant delight of the inner Self.* Entrance into the process or journey to this full expansion of Shakti is the purpose of the receipt of *authentic* Shaktipat. This *journey* is what we refer to in Nityananda Shaktipat Yoga as the *Shaktipat Kriya Process.*

This Grace-bestowing power is transmitted by an authentic Shaktipat Guru to awaken Kundalini (dormant spiritual energy, dormant spiritual awareness), and to revolutionize one's meditation practice and spiritual life. Those who have had a lapse in their spiritual practice or feel the need for additional support, also return to receive this transmission of Grace-bestowing power.

Understanding What Shaktipat Really Is

Contrary to what some high-profile spiritual teachers say (who have never received Shaktipat, by the way), Kundalini is not awakened through jumping around, rebounding or playing sports. If this were so, most of the NFL would be populated with yogis who want to attain permanent spiritual transformation. And we know this is not the case!

Shaktipat does not occur during moments of intense activity either. In fact, that's like saying that someone who does shots at a bar, one after the other, for an extended period of time will awaken his/her Kundalini. Or that wild sex for a day will do so, with controlled concentration. Or that an intense, controlled focus on stealing money by hacking bank servers will also awaken Kundalini.

Ha! Even a child knows better. And yet, under pressure of embarrassment, due to becoming one of those 'go to' Internet experts with no experience of Shaktipat, such 'spiritual teachers' are making it up as they go.

No Effort Required?

One mistake that many yogis make in their understanding of Shaktipat is that, after its receipt, there is nothing else to do except, perhaps, meditate. Within this understanding is the false notion that no particular instructed practice or ongoing leadership in the spiritual journey is required – that one day at some point in the future, the state of Liberation will just dawn on its own, or by the will of the individual. Would that this be true! Then there would be no particular effort on our part to attain anything lasting – and no discipline required in doing so.

Of course, this is not true and this is where so many get it wrong. This useless understanding is also the cause of so many who have never received authentic Shaktipat and never followed a Shaktipat Guru, who then claim to give it. Unfortunately, today this is the environment in which Shaktipat has been reduced to a questionable commodity – with comparisons to suspicious 'spontaneous awakenings' and the use of hallucinogenic drugs (disguised as 'ceremonial' in nature) that promise instant enlightenment. How unfortunate to be robbed of the true Shaktipat experience in such ways!

As my Gurudev used to say, "Milk exists naturally in cows, but one still has to make the effort to get the milk out. Diamonds exist naturally in the Earth, but there is still something one has to do to get them out." In the Shiva Sutras, Shivaji states, "Udyamo Bhairava" - extended, vigilant effort is itself God. So, the initial receipt of authentic

Shaktipat is *only the beginning* of true Shaktipat, setting the stage for what must come next.

Which Would You Rather Have: A Passing Glimpse, Or A Permanent Realization of The Self?

So, if extended, vigilant effort is required after the receipt of the transmission of Shaktipat, why is the receipt of Shaktipat called 'the easy means?' What's easy about it?

My Shri Gurudev often repeated the words of so many Sages of our lineage: "We've been going in the wrong direction for so long, attaching ourselves to objects of sense in so many hopeless pursuits – seeking Joy and Happiness where they are not – looking outside, outside, outside for it in all the wrong places. This has become our perpetual habit, our ritual bath."

As I'm sure you are aware from your own life experience thus far, in many cases, old habits are very hard to break. People love their 'comfort zones' that they have developed out of the choices they have made over so many years and lifetimes. And people love 'good news' about their bad habits. Literally, the 'ocean liner' of limiting desire and craving has been traveling at high speed in the wrong direction for so long that it must now be brought to a complete halt in order to change direction.

Here I'm speaking of the hot pursuit of worldliness, the ferocious pursuit of comfort, security and reward – in the hope of possessing people, places and things on some level – in the hope of being completed by something or someone – based on the false notion that you lack something that now needs to be pursued at all costs and by any means necessary.

Some people try to turn this ocean liner around, but the Captain of that boat does not know any other direction in which to take it. Add to all of this the tremendous amount of distraction we face today – the distraction of constant stimulation and the pursuit of instant gratification embodied in attachment, attraction and aversion. The previous generation did not have the challenge of such distractions as we face today. And our ancestors did not suffer these distractions at all (as a result, they were so much more disciplined).

So, why is authentic Shaktipat the easy means and what's 'easy' about it? The fact is the 'ocean liner' I speak of above *cannot be turned around.* As I said, the Captain of that boat knows no other direction in which to take it. So, it must be *abandoned* for the boat of the Sadguru, the only boat that will take you to that distant shore of the Self! The Sadguru is himself that boat, being the Captain who knows the destination because he has ferried people across the treacherous ocean of worldliness to that destination and knows it well - because that destination is the Shaktipat Guru's dwelling place – the abode of the true Heart – the Supreme Self.

In a sea of worldliness in which so many are drowning, will you attempt to leap off that ocean liner of despair into the treacherous waters in which you have observed so many others drown – with no life raft, no life vest, sharks in the water and no land in sight?! Authentic Shaktipat is the *easy means* to halt that racing ship long enough for you to be rescued off it safely, so that you can easily climb into the right boat!

Here's The Rest of What Authentic Shaktipat Is

Once in the right boat, the boat of the Guru, headed in the perfect direction, you have to *stay in the boat!* Herein lies the challenge that requires the ongoing leadership and companionship of an experienced Siddha Guru – what we refer to as the Shaktipat Kriya Process or Sadhana.

We have so many past and present Karmas to face (that ocean liner). My Gurudev said that Sadhana is like a bird, in that birds need two wings to fly. The first is the tremendous Grace of the Shaktipat Sadguru and the second is your loving Grace, embodied in your ongoing, vigilant effort at Sadhana.

Without your Grace being extended in this manner, by putting forth self-effort in the manner instructed, God's Grace that is embodied in the form of the living Guru cannot rescue you. Why? Because you won't stay in the boat without the kind of self-effort that is *imbued with spiritual discipline*. And, for most of us, spiritual discipline does not come naturally. It has to be carefully taught to us.

Therefore, your Grace is also required. So, Shaktipat is both the way to get you into the right boat that is headed to that distant shore of the Self, and *the means to keep you in that boat that is taking you to Freedom*. It requires a steady effort for you to stay in the boat of the Sadguru. Your first class seat on the 'ocean liner' of worldliness is what you have pined for all your life, even knowing, at times, that it has been taking you in the wrong direction. There are so many enjoying the pleasures on that ocean liner that you have come to believe it's the right boat for you. You see, you've been on that ship for so long without realizing that you've been riding the Titanic – a ship destined to sink!

So, yes, we are talking about a change in lifestyle! The lifestyle you have led is the underlying cause of your 'madness.' You've filled your head with all kinds of notions beliefs and habits that will take time to break. Changing those old, vicious habits (karmic patterns) means you have to stay in the boat of the Guru. The original transmission of Shaktipat gets you safely into that boat. The rest of Shaktipat is the process that keeps you in it.

Only this will ensure that, over time, you evolve into a permanent, *tested and verified* state of the Highest, the Self, rather than just experiencing Shaktipat as a passing glimpse that, like so many, you may even take for granted. Shri Gurudev Bhagawan Nityananda of Ganeshpuri has said:

"One must live in the world like common people. Once established in infinite consciousness, one becomes silent and, knowing all, goes about as if knowing nothing. Although he may be doing many things in several places, he outwardly appears as if he is simply a witness to life - like a spectator at the cinema. He is unaffected by events, whether pleasant or unpleasant. The ability to forget everything and remain detached is the highest state possible."

And in another of His utterances…

"The only thing required for spiritual growth is detachment from worldly pleasures. If you don't listen to this, you will fail in the end. The thoughtless state, the state of detachment, is the highest state. How can there be desire in the state of detachment? It is not the world the yogi gives up. It is desire for worldly sense pleasure. The true yogi is full and content whether he/she is a pauper or a rich person. If pleasurable things come your way, experience them, but never go looking. Always be content in yourself wherever you are and whatever your circumstances."

Contemplate Bhagawan Nityananda's words for just a few minutes. What state is being described and how can you hope to achieve it without the necessary leadership – the leadership in your steady self-effort that is ripe with the most useful methods for attaining the goal?

So, contrary to what many believe or have been told when receiving what is not Shaktipat; Shaktipat doesn't end at the transmission of God's Grace bestowing power. So, understand what authentic Shaktipat really is.

Spontaneous Meditation

Authentic Shaktipat begins with the transmission of the highest spiritual energy that, gradually, makes meditation more spontaneous. You are able to be fully present in the moment more and more often – fully present with your own Peace and Joy. For some, this state unfolds very quickly after Shaktipat initiation. For others, it takes a while. This is due to differences in people's Karmas. However, if the original transmission of Grace was authentic, for those who stay in the Shaktipat Guru's boat, spontaneous Meditation on a regular basis is inevitable.

Shaktipat also invokes the inner healing process that purifies the heart, the body and *all* the subtle spiritual energy centers (provided one stays in the boat of the Guru, rather than jumping out of that boat to swim back to a sinking ship). Over time, this purification allows you to embrace a *spiritual lifestyle* of *Joy*, *Content* and *Well-being of your entire being.*

Authentic Shaktipat deepens and accelerates your spiritual practice in this way. After this awakening is received, a purification process begins whereby, over time and with regular spiritual practice, the fully awakened Kundalini Shakti pierces and purifies all of the subtle energy centers within the physical and subtle bodies.

Over time and with vigilant practice of the Guru's instruction, this awakening leads to a person becoming completely established in his/her own Joy, with the constant awareness and experience of the Ultimate Reality inside and everywhere.

By the nurturing of this full Shakti awakening through daily spiritual practice and a lifestyle change, *as instructed*, the student experiences an inner unfolding of awareness that leads to states of higher and higher conscious awareness of the Ultimate Reality. Gradually you secure the Bliss, Joy, Peace, Happiness, and Well-Being that is your birthright. In our school, we have documented this transformation in students over a period of many years.

If You Could Do It The Easy Way Or The Hard Way, Which Would You Choose?

We are, at our core, all energetic beings. In daily mundane life, nothing can function without *energy. In spiritual life it is the same.* My Shri Gurudev opened the floodgates of vitality for me by leading me to become established in what I refer to as *the energy substratum*, that Divine Conscious Energy or Shakti that even Quantum Physics and the science of Epigenetics now fully embrace as *the energy field*. The Sages of steady wisdom of our lineage refer to this as the substratum of all things.

Start by contemplating the following, undeniable Truth, for this is not only the easy way but it is the only way.

The Importance of Lineage

The poet Saint Kabir has said, "Guru Janam Janam Ki Atak Koli." It means "The Guru has freed you from being stuck for many lifetimes." This freedom comes by way of the Shaktipat Sadguru actually burning away the Karmas you have created that keep you bound to ignorance. An authentic Shaktipat Guru is able to accomplish this *only by the power of an unbroken lineage of such beings that the Guru serves.*

This is why, when it comes to Shaktipat and Sadhana, lineage is essential. The living Master must consistently please his/her lineage in order to constantly invoke the power that, combined with the Grace of your own self-effort, *burns away all that you are not – your Karmas.*

This is why my Shri Gurudev emphasized great caution in choosing a Guru to receive Shaktipat from. He would say that, if such a being wears colored robes and professes to give Shaktipat, but has never served another Master or lineage, is he a Guru or a dyer?! My Baba would also warn us that the false Guru market is growing exponentially because the false disciple market is so large!

For these reasons, when considering the receipt of the greatest gift on the planet – Shaktipat – and the leadership that must follow, be sure you receive Shaktipat from one who is in a lineage of Shaktipat Sadgurus. Such a being must have served a Shaktipat Guru in this lineage, *over an extended period of time* – **a matter of years**, not weeks or months!

Again, this is so because such a being must have been completely erased and molded by his/her own Guru. *This is the only way in which Shaktipat Gurus attain the power necessary to burn the Karmas that cause you to be stuck, lifetime after lifetime.*

So, investigate this carefully. If the 'guru' has no lineage that he/she has served, no master that he/she served for many years, *then do not follow.* You will not receive authentic Shaktipat from such a person, nor will such a person be able to consistently give the direct experience of what he/she instructs.

Test The Guru

After the initiation of Shaktipat that fully awakens the dormant Kundalini, there is a journey of unfolding that begins. In Nityananda Shaktipat Yoga, we like to say that this is a journey to retrace our steps back to God. It is an inevitable journey dictated by the sacred law that governs this place – a free evolution of beings who God sends here.

This unfolding is a nurturing of the fully awakened Kundalini. It is like a gardener or farmer who has planted seeds for a wonderful bounty of crops. That garden, those crops need to be nurtured to harvest. Sadhana, the Shaktipat Kriya Process that begins upon the receipt of Shaktipat, is very much like this.

This unfolding is supported by a daily spiritual practice and discipline that is taught by a living Shaktipat Sadguru. Indeed, this unfolding has many obstacles of karmic tendencies opposing it. This is why we need leadership in this process. And that leadership has to be strong, true and based on both personal experience and the collective experience of a lineage that has made the same journey.

So, you don't want to follow just anyone in the unfolding of your Sadhana. Instead, you want to be sure that you are with the right one. This requires that, as you begin this journey, you also test the Guru, before fully embracing this leadership for the unfolding and nurturing of the awakened Kundalini.

In Nityananda Shaktipat Yoga, the means to test the Guru has been taught and supported down through the ages in our lineage of Siddhas – the Sages of Steady Wisdom – the spiritually-perfected Love Beings. The steps to testing the Guru are:

1. You must have experiences of peace, joy, love and strength while in the company of the Guru and by following the instruction of such a Guru. And you have to have inner experiences of the awakened Kundalini, upon the receipt of Shaktipat. These experiences may be subtle or blatant, but they must take place. Your experiences should indicate to you that, if you continue to keep the company of the Guru and follow his instruction, your mind will become quieter and quieter, your joy will increase, and fear will be erased from your being. Peace and Love should follow, and your longing to know God should increase regularly. The beneficial experiences others share who keep the company of the Guru, along with your observation of their transformation should also be considered. But that does not replace the fact that *you must have experiences.*

2. In your own direct observation, the Guru's speech and actions should be pure, dharmic and full of the intention to serve the spiritual needs of you and other students/devotees. Such a Guru should speak regularly of his/her experiences of his own Guru. The Guru's behavior should clearly indicate his love for and devotion to his own Guru and the lineage. Such a Guru's speech and actions should be free of attachment, attraction, aversion and limiting desires and cravings that are hallmarks of worldliness.

3. The Guru's speech, actions and instruction must be supported by the scriptures and sacred texts that comprise the Wisdom, the utterances of the Sages of Steady Wisdom of the Guru's lineage. Such texts should be made available for followers to examine and study, to support this test of the Guru. The

Guru's leadership should be in complete alignment with these scriptures and sacred texts.

In our lineage, the above is what is known as the 3-test of the Guru. It has been used by many beings to test their Guru when taking up Sadhana. This test requires that you give yourself time to begin following the Guru's instruction for your Sadhana.

You need time to be able to test what you are taught in the laboratory of your own existence. You need time to have experiences of what takes place when you follow the instruction vigilantly, as compared to what happens when you don't. You need time to journal these experiences as a scientist would, so that you can determine whether or not you have performed the test of the Guru *to your satisfaction*.

For most, this is a period of 6-24 months. But that is not a hard and fast rule, *as a lot depends on how long it takes for you to actually take up and follow instruction.*

The Shaktipat Kriya Process

After the initial receipt of Shaktipat from an authentic Shaktipat Guru, the *Sadhana* that solidifies the unfolding of the awakened Kundalini to realization of its fullest potential begins in earnest. This process of unfolding is best secured in the bond of power between the Devotee and the Shaktipat Sadguru. This is the *Shaktipat Kriya Process* in which everything you are not is rooted out and addressed in a way that you become increasingly and consciously aware of:

- Your Karmic tendencies that are the obstacle to your permanent spiritual transformation and Liberation.

- All the ways in which you refuse to let go of these tendencies, thereby concealing your true nature from yourself and concealing the experience of the highest Bliss of the Self.

- The steps and instruction you must follow to rid yourself of these false leanings and tendencies, beginning with the ego idea that causes you to live in a state of fear.

Just as your bathroom mirror may reveal how you really look without primping and makeup, the Shaktipat Kriya Process has its foundation in a similar mirror. This is called the mirror of the Guru, and its power is unfathomable. It is the root of all expanding spiritual awareness and permanent spiritual transformation. Sadhana is based on having this mirror of the Sadguru's Shakti as the outside agent that reflects back to you what you cannot see without the mirror - just like in the case of what is revealed to you when you look into your bathroom mirror right after waking up in the morning.

Again, the Shakti of the living Shaktipat Guru acts like a huge mirror, reflecting both a person's useful and useless tendencies back to him/her. The Guru's Shakti, in the form of that fully awakened Kundalini, will also bring up and make evident tendencies and weaknesses that are lurking just below the surface of the student's conscious awareness. In this way, the student/devotee is always given a clue as to where he/she is at in the moment.

For example, in close physical proximity to the living Siddha Guru, and also in that Guru's school or center, if your ego is ablaze (limiting, impure perceptions and emotions) those are going to be reflected back to you, often in stark contrast to where you think you are at. Additionally, this is also the Sadguru's challenge to you.

Another very important point is this: It must be understood that the Shaktipat Sadguru *does not* take away your pain and suffering. *The Guru's job is to show you the root cause of your suffering and help you remove that root cause.* Therefore, students who see the Guru as a "dumping ground" for their suffering are not able to go the distance. Such people usually come to a skewed vision of the Guru that forces them off the path.

Without the Blessing and Grace of this mirror, it is not possible for you to become aware of the karmic leanings and tendencies that are holding you back. Likewise, one needs a very strong spiritual witnessing awareness to harness the bond of power in the mirror of the Guru, in a way that you learn to let go of these useless and binding impurities so that they can be rooted out permanently.

Indeed, it is this miraculous mirror that forms the foundation for your ever-expanding spiritual witnessing awareness that is so necessary in Sadhana. This ever-expanding witnessing awareness is the unfolding of Kundalini.

Shaktipat FAQ

The following is taken from a live Q&A program in which Kedarji was asked questions about Shaktipat and Sadhana.

Question: What is Authentic Shaktipat?

Answer:

If you go online today, it appears that everyone and their brother is a Shaktipat-giver. These people make it sound like every energetic experience is Shaktipat.

And particularly, in certain places on the planet, they have made a business of this now. Unfortunately, Shaktipat has gone the route of American yoga. When Yoga was first offered, it was understood that Yoga is a transformational path to experiencing the highest in you, the Self. *Yoga actually means the transformation of limited human awareness into Divine Awareness of the Ultimate Reality – the energy substratum of everything – Divine Conscious Energy or Shakti*, but that's not what you see on the sign for the yoga studio today.

In fact, many years ago when I was taking a course in how to run a healing business, they were talking about yoga, and they told us "Never say Hatha Yoga (the type that is popular today), never say anything else, just say yoga when you run your business." So, *yoga has become commercialized*, and Shaktipat has now gone the same route, and it's a big commercial.

Healers have now jumped into the act, putting up websites that say they give Shaktipat. People who have studied a few hours of Reiki, without long-term mentoring, or have simply read a book on it say, "I'm a Shaktipat-giver." Anyone who has any energetic experience says, "Oh, I received Shaktipat." In most cases, this is false. So, what is Shaktipat then?

First of all, there's nothing wrong with healing. There's nothing wrong with giving energy to another individual that you have the power to extend. So, I'm not negating any of these things. I'm just saying *that's not Shaktipat*. Healers give you energy. Shaktipat awakens an energy you already have. This is the first thing you have to understand. *This energy has two aspects.*

At the base of your spine, in the Muladhara chakra, there is the second aspect of an energy you're already used to using (immanent aspect). The energy you use to concentrate, to focus on objects of sense, on people, places and things - when you're able to do that well, you call that *concentration*. Concentration is taught from a very young age. But there is another aspect to that same energy that lays dormant within your being at the base of your spine, until it is fully awakened.

The dormant aspect of that energy is the *transcendental* aspect of One Supreme Intelligence. This is a sleeping awareness that is then awakened through authentic Shaktipat. In its state of sleeping, it's known as Kundalini. It is awakened by a Shaktipat Guru who has been authorized to awaken the Kundalini by another Shaktipat Guru. *This is the first thing you must understand.* We exist in this Kali Yuga age where there is so much misinformation and disinformation. Any kind of teacher puts a shingle out and says, "I'm doing this, I have the power to do this" when they've only read a book, for example.

Understand that Authentic Shaktipat is what I'm speaking about now. Authentic Shaktipat can only be given by a Siddha Guru who is also a Shaktipat Guru *in a lineage of such beings.* Here we make that distinction for one reason only – there are Sadgurus who do not give Shaktipat. So, this is why we say, "…must also be a Shaktipat Guru."

Even today on this earth plane, a Siddha Guru is very rare. *A Shaktipat Guru is even more rare.* One who gives Shaktipat has to have been authorized to do so by his or her Guru, whom that person served – **not just for a week, a month or a couple of months – for**

years. My Shri Gurudev used to say, *"Only the one who obeys can command."*

Now, you already know this. Suppose you need heart surgery. Do you go to the person who says, "I'm going to learn how to operate on hearts by operating on yours."? No! That would be a ridiculous notion. Let's suppose you're in trouble with the law, and now you need a good attorney. Do you go to the paralegal who says, "I've never tried a case."? No! That would be stupidity. *It's no different in spiritual life, particularly with respect to Shaktipat.*

Authentic Shaktipat is given by one who has obeyed a Guru, one who has been a disciple of a Shaktipat Guru for many years – to the point where that Master authorized this person to give Shaktipat and extended the Grace and the full amount of Shakti to do so. The full amount means that such disciples of a Shaktipat Guru, once authorized, are able to transmit the Grace-bestowing power of God without ever becoming depleted of their own Shakti.

This is what full amount means: that no matter how many people such beings transmit this Grace-bestowing power to, their own Shakti, their own energy is never depleted. Only one who has stored up the full amount can do it. When do such disciples know they've stored up the full amount? *When their Guru tells them, either outwardly or inwardly; that's how they know.*

This is why authentic Shaktipat-givers *are in a lineage of Shaktipat Gurus.* Do not seek Shaktipat from any other beings. A healer may be able to heal you of illness by dint of that person's combined spiritual merit of many past lives. Healers may be able to heal you, and in doing so, may even burn some of your karmas, temporarily; **but that is not Shaktipat.**

You may experience beings where, in their company, they're able to transmit some energy to you. It is possible that there's an energy exchange, *but this is not Shaktipat.* And here's why: make certain you're listening very carefully… **Shaktipat has a very specific intention. Upon the receipt of Shaktipat, there begins what is known as Sadhana, what, in Nityananda Shaktipat Yoga is called the *Shaktipat Kriya Process.***

The intention of Shaktipat is to release you from the bondage of ignorance by securing your permanent spiritual transformation and Liberation. That's the intention in which it is given. **Therefore, the one giving it also has to be able to lead you through this Shaktipat Kriya Process over an extended period of time, for as long as it takes to liberate you.** This is the difference that makes the difference.

Sadhana begins upon the receipt of this highest spiritual initiation. Therefore, Shaktipat is the greatest gift you can ever receive because it begins a spontaneous unfolding of your spiritual awareness. The dormant Kundalini is the awareness that is sleeping. It's awakened just like lighting an unlit candle with one that's already lit; there's just this leap, and it's subtle but so profound!

You have to understand this: *Shaktipat is a matter of subtleties, not a matter of blatant things like the sky opening up and you hear the voice of Charlton Heston as Ben-Hur or Moses saying, "Come to me."* Some people watch too many movies. **Although, if with the right one, people can and do have very strong, initial** experiences of the receipt of this Grace-bestowing power of God, this is not all that Shaktipat is about. *Shaktipat is all about the subtleties.*

Also, understand that, if it is authentic Shaktipat, there is an intention that the Guru then delivers on. **And that is the process that roots out all of the karmic tendencies that are the obstacles to your permanent spiritual transformation and Liberation. Therefore, Shaktipat is an unfolding process in which you engage ongoing, spiritual leadership from one who is an adept in this regard, due to having served another Siddha Guru for many years.**

Only this is Shaktipat; and you should only receive this Highest transmission of the Grace-bestowing power of God from a Siddha Guru where there is a proved ability to lead you through this Shaktipat Kriya Process.

Question: So, once you know you have a Guru who can give you Shaktipat, and then you receive Shaktipat, does it last forever, or does it have to be, let's just say, tuned up for a better term in use?

Answer:

This is a very good question. That depends on *your effort.* The truth is, if you're with a Sadguru, a Shaktipat Guru, it's always raining Grace. Such beings can only give Grace, and this is my experience and that of my Shri Gurudev, and his Guru before him. Sadgurus who are Shaktipat Gurus can only give

Grace. Now, will you embrace that Grace or sabotage it? This is the question.

This is also why you need leadership. You can't arrive at a place that you've never seen, never experienced and don't know anything about; for that, you need to be led. Let's say, as an example, you grab a cab in New York City to go uptown and you want to make sure you're going to Riverdale and not Harlem. But you've never been to either place. You have to rely on the cab driver, don't you? You have to get a cabbie who knows the difference between Harlem and Riverdale and is actually going to take you to Riverdale and not drop you in the South Bronx by an abandoned building, just because the taxi driver didn't know. So, what does that mean?

You need a particular taxi driver, don't you? You need a driver who knows all of uptown New York City and knows to take you to Riverdale and not the South Bronx in the demilitarized zone, right? That's a specific cab driver. So, here, you need a specific Guru for the same reason.

You hit on a very important point because one of the roles of a Shaktipat Guru is to consistently stay after you to ensure that you're nurturing this wonderful, full Shakti Awakening, and that you are performing the self-effort necessary to nurture that awakening. Can the fully awakened Kundalini become dormant again? Yes, to a certain extent, it can, if you don't nurture it.

Consider this example: Let's say you have this wonderful bed of flowers. They need watering and regular care. If you never water those flowers and never remove any weeds growing in the flowerbed, the flowers are going to die. However, the seed will remain. This is a perfect analogy for Shaktipat.

If you don't water that incredible gift of Grace to cause it to increase and to increase and to increase with the love of your self-effort, it will become dormant; but the seed will remain. This is why we also say Shaktipat never really goes to waste. The seed will be there, but the manifestation of that seed in such a way that you can use it to completely expand your spiritual awareness will not remain unless there is effort on your part to follow the instruction to nurture that awakening, so that the Kundalini continues to rise.

What is rising? Your spiritual awareness. Your self-effort, as instructed by the Sadguru is offered so that your spiritual, witnessing awareness continues to expand and expand and expand, rather than contracting back to that original ignorance for which you received Shaktipat to address. So, yes, after Shaktipat, the Kundalini can become dormant in this way, and we see this. In my Gurudev's time, there were people who came and went. Some of those people treated Shaktipat like taking drugs. They wouldn't follow the instruction completely, they'd go to an intensive, get Shaktipat – get high. For, it is the best high. Then they'd run off and engage in all kinds of contracting activity.

And then they would say to Baba (because my Gurudev was giving intensives every weekend), "Baba, I'll see you next month." And they'd come back and they'd be completely dried out and they'd look horrible, and they'd say, "Ok, I'm taking the intensive again." So, they'd go get a little bit more energy and they'd run away and say, "Okay, I'll see you in three months because I'm going to party in Europe. I'm going to hit the clubs every night. I'm just going to waste all my Shakti. I'm going to have sex twice a day and I'm just going to waste all the Shakti and do drugs." And, again, they would come back completely dried out and say, "Okay, I'm here to take another intensive." This *is not* the way to proceed.

What happened to those people is, eventually, my Baba took Mahasamadhi (passed from the body for the last time). Now where are they going to go every week for Shaktipat? There are very few lineage holders now remaining, and Kedarji does not give intensives every week. Furthermore, for people who are just treating it as a drug, you can only sabotage Grace for so long.

You have a rosebush that's flowering, but you're not taking care of the bush; you're not weeding out the weeds, you're not watering the bush, but you're still taking the roses off because you like the roses. You just don't like taking care of the bush, but you love the roses.

Eventually, that bush is going to die. You'll get the roses out, only for so long, and now it stops producing beautiful roses, because you haven't been taking care of it.

So, this does happen, for some, with respect to Shaktipat. And people do engage in this kind of behavior, but again, this is why the Sadguru exists, to lead you over those kinds of hurdles.

Question: My second part of that was, as you talked about Shaktipat, you talked about

surrendering. Can you explain what surrendering is in this approach? What are you surrendering?

Answer:

You're surrendering the limitation of your ego, and that's it. But that's a big 'it,' isn't it? Because the ego is your lover. Then, if you make the ego your jilted lover, the ego is going to stalk you, so expect it. That's why you need the order of protection – the order of protection is your Guru. That's why you need that order, because the ego is going to stalk you. The harder you try to root it out, the more it's going to stalk you. It gets subtler and subtler, so that's what you're surrendering, and the ego has to be surrendered completely.

There is no need to change the clothes you wear. There is no need to go on long monthly fasts. There is no need to take pilgrimages 10-15,000 miles away to certain temples. These temples are beautiful and there is nothing wrong with taking pilgrimages. Sometimes making such an effort helps to invoke Bhakti, longing – and that's a good thing. But there's no *need* to do it when you have a Shaktipat Guru at the helm of your boat. There's no need to go to confession on Sundays. You don't need any of these things to be Liberated in the moment or to expand on that experience.

The only thing you need to realize the Self, your True Nature, is to surrender the ego, the false notion of being the body, the mind, the senses.

Like I said, the ego has been your lover for centuries, so you need a third party to help you root it out.

When you go to therapy, that's why you go – because there is a third, unbiased party in the therapist. You've been in relationships for a while, you have a breakdown, now you talk to your lover and you say, "Okay, let's go to therapy. We need some help." It's the same with the ego. With the Siddha Guru, now you're going into a kind of therapy. This is the Guru's therapy. When it comes to surrendering the ego, the Guru is the therapist that you're going to see.

Your intention is to break up, but your ego doesn't know that yet. You're getting a little slick with the ego, you're saying, "Okay my beloved ego, let's go to therapy. So, the ego thinks, "Ok, maybe she still likes me." Your intention is to get rid of that ego, but you don't tell your ego-lover yet. You tell the therapist first.

Ever been in this situation with an intimate relationship? So, the therapist says, "Ok, husband, step out of the room," and then the therapist talks to you separately. This is done in all relationship counseling. The therapist talks to you together and then talks to you individually. So, the husband steps out and the therapist says, "Ok wife, now, tell me the truth, tell me how you really feel." "Well, how I really feel is I'm done with this."

So, this is why we need the Maha (great) therapist in the Sadguru, so that we can be done with the ego idea that we have made our lover for so long. So, this is what you do. You take the ego to the therapist and the therapist is the Guru. You say, "Pssst…" and the Guru says, "Don't worry, I'll handle it." Sometimes that's the way you have to be with your ego - leave it on a need-to-know basis. In this way, you surrender the ego that is the false notion of individuality. Then you can realize your true worth.

But it is very difficult, if not impossible, to surrender the ego without the Grace of the Shaktipat Blessing. This is why I took an authentic Shaktipat Guru.

Question: What is the proper way to prepare for Shaktipat? How does one know that he/she is ready?

Answer:

The moment that you have the desire to truly know God, to have a personal relationship with God, that's when you're ready. The moment you are aware that you have that desire. Because most have this desire and they're not yet aware of it. But the moment that you're aware, even if it's just the question, "Who am I?" Even if it's just the understanding there must be something greater than this; don't yet know what it is, but I want something greater than just this daily mundane life. At that moment, you're ready.

Chapter 4
Experience Shares of
Those Who Have Received
Shaktipat From Kedarji

In blind surveys and case studies conducted over the last 17 years, our program offering has been proved to deliver results beyond the expectations of our students.

Vital Statistics

For every Nityananda Shaktipat Yoga event, when surveyed at the end of the event, participants are asked, "Do you feel more calm and at peace, with a quieter mind now, as compared to when you first came in the door?" 100% of those surveyed answered YES.

In blind surveys, 2 out of every 3 people report that:

- While being led in our Witness Consciousness Centering methods, they experienced a profound sense of Peace and the 'no mind' state in under 3 minutes.
- Their sense of content and happiness increased in the 90-minutes that they attended a program.
- They experienced a state that they recognized to be beyond the mind, body, the senses and the emotions.
- As a result of practicing the methods they are taught by Kedarji, they experience that they are more confident that they can access the

inner strength necessary to take on life's challenges.

- Keeping the company of Kedarji has opened their hearts and freed them from contracting emotions, restless thoughts and attachments to worldliness.

Shaktipat Blessing Retreats

In exit surveys and post-intensive follow up surveys, 96% of all people who have taken our weekend Shaktipat Blessing Retreat report that they have become anchored in a life-changing set of experiences that are the clear proof that they received a profound spiritual blessing of Grace that is undeniable.

Of this group, 90% report that, after a 3-year period, post-retreat, they are continuing to apply the principles and practices they learned in these weekend Shaktipat Blessing Retreats with Kedarji, and are experiencing the following results:

- Increasingly permanent states of peace of mind.
- Increased longing to experience the Bliss of the Inner Self.
- Increasing experiences of Joy and Content as they go about their daily mundane activities.
- An ever-increasing, heightened spiritual witnessing awareness that allows them to share Love without conditions, without making distinctions or relishing in the false notion of duality.
- The increased ability to engage their lives without becoming attached to or experiencing aversion to people, places and things.

- The steadily increasing ability to take on life's challenges while remaining centered in their experience of inner Peace and Joy.
- A sharper mind and increased inspiration for daily living.
- Relief from chronic health symptoms.

Of this same group, 80% report that, after a 5-year period, post-retreat, they are continuing to apply the principles and practices they learned in these weekend Shaktipat Blessing Retreats with Kedarji to experience the following results, in addition to those stated above:

- The ability to maintain a heightened spiritual witnessing awareness, steeped in the experience of inner Peace and Bliss that is not reduced by worldly distractions or the fluctuation of situations and circumstances.
- A purified heart that is open to giving and receiving without bartering needs for wants.
- A deepening experience of Love without distinctions in all their interactions.
- A quiet mind that dissolves in Bliss and Inner Peace.

In addition, there is a group of disciples in our spiritual community who have been participating in our programs and providing support to our school for a period of 10-18 years. In all that time, we have monitored and recorded their progress in Sadhana under the leadership of Kedarji. These disciples have made progress that exceeds what is stated in the above statistics.

Students of Kedarji
Share Their Experiences

The following is a transcription taken from a video that appears on the home page of our web site.

Interviewer: I have a few questions. This question goes to Ben and Kambra. In your experience, what is Shaktipat?

Ben T.: Shaktipat—the word, according to my understanding—means "descent of Grace." But I don't think that really conveys the magnitude of what I've experienced Shaktipat to be. Prior to receiving Shaktipat, I absolutely was not a spiritual person. But I did do some seeking, and eventually, I came across Sadguru Kedarji's website, and I did receive Shaktipat from Sadguru Kedarji. And in my experience, Shaktipat is the key that opened up the door to spirituality for me.

Kambra M.: Shaktipat is the beginning of the most important and truly transformational journey of my life. It is an unfolding of my spiritual awareness, and an awakening of an energy that I already have. And it helps me realize my true nature and also see where I am hiding my understanding and realization of my true nature.

We are all joy, peace, content, bliss, love, but due to so many distractions in our world, in our everyday mundane lives, we've gotten really good at hiding that truth from ourselves and forgetting that that is our true nature. So, the blessing of Shaktipat is helping me to gain awareness of all the subtle ways in which I hide my true nature from myself. And it's showing me that I can lead that happy and fearless and free life that I've always wanted to lead and always tried so hard to achieve in so many ways.

But the thing is there is nothing to achieve. It's all about simply gaining more and more awareness of the subtleties of how I hold myself back. And the true beauty of Shaktipat is that it's not about a quick fix or a short-term experience. The benefits of Shaktipat can have an infinite, long-term, long-lasting effect when I put forth the self-effort to nurture and properly cultivate this blessing of true Grace.

Interviewer: Thank you. This question goes to David, Deana, and Shanti. It seems that there's so many approaches out there. Why did you choose to receive Shaktipat?

Shanti H.: I know for me, I received Shaktipat because my life was falling apart. I had participated in different spiritual approaches before coming to Sadguru Kedarji. And, you know, the Christian tradition, I was involved in a spiritualist church for a period of time, and none of these things ever gave me any lasting, permanent spiritual transformation.

And that's really what I was looking for. And none of these other approaches gave that to me. Something was always missing. And when I met Sadguru Kedarji and I received Shaktipat, that bestowal of Grace is what promised to lead me to experience permanent spiritual transformation. If I just follow the instructions that I'm given for Sadhana, for my daily spiritual practices...and it's not a blind faith. It's an actual science here.

So, we don't do or believe anything just blindly. We're given the methods and the practices that are proven to work, to deliver us to that experience of inner peace and joy and happiness. And it works. And I have the direct experience of that.

Interviewer: Thank you. Deana?

Deana T.: Yes, there are so many paths, and I think I went down all of them and tried everything. I was a spiritual seeker, a spiritual junkie. And, in my spiritual journey, I'd ask a lot of questions. What is the meaning of life? What is my life's purpose? Why am I here? And as I started to go down that spiritual journey a little bit further, I added the question in: And why am I so stuck in life?

Because I was doing everything that I could at that time to find relief and to find some peace, to heal traumatic relationships, to just be calm and centered. And when I met Sadguru Kedarji and I came to a program, he offered a method to us during the program, and I had this very direct experience of my mind stopping and becoming quiet. And that really intrigued me. So, I decided to receive Shaktipat from that experience, because I really wanted to know more of this approach and what Shaktipat was about, and exactly what Sadguru Kedarji had to offer me.

Interviewer: Thank you. David?

David G.: I chose to receive Shaktipat because it's what I had heard was the essential key to leading a spiritual life. I've been a spiritual seeker since I was a teenager. I read as many books as I could find on yoga and meditation and mysticism. I've studied with a number of different teachers. And two things kept coming up in a lot of my studies and my seeking: the need for Shaktipat, and the need for a genuine Sadguru. So, that's why I chose to receive Shaktipat,

and my yearning and longing paid off, and I found
both Shaktipat and a genuine Sadguru.

Interviewer: Amazing. This question is also for you
three. I just want to follow up. Is Shaktipat received
for the purpose of healing or any fulfillment of
worldly mundane desires?

David G.: No, I don't believe that's the case. There
are a lot of different offerings in the world, a lot of
different energies being offered. Some for healing,
some for finding your soulmate, some for improving
your financial circumstances. And I've actually
worked with some teachers who've taught some of
these paths that have those things as goals. They're all
predicated on changing something outside of yourself
in order to achieve happiness.
And Shaktipat is not like that at all. Shaktipat is about
turning inward to experience the Bliss of the Self. To
experience a state that's not dependent in any way on
anything outside of yourself.

Interviewer: Thank you. Shanti?

Shanti H.: That's not the point of Shaktipat.
Shaktipat is to begin to allow yourself to be able to
experience your true nature of bliss and Love. And
healing of illnesses or diseases, or improvement in
mundane life can sometimes happen, but those are
side benefits. That's not the purpose of Shaktipat.
And I know, in my own experience, I have received
or have experienced healing of an illness. I was healed
of an "incurable" neurological condition. But that was
just a side benefit of Shaktipat. The real goal is to
experience your true nature.

Interviewer: Thank you. This question is for all of you, but I'd like to start with Kambra first. I understand that Shaktipat is the transmission of the Grace-bestowing power of God. In your experience, how did this Grace connected to karmas make authentic Shaktipat the difference that really makes the difference?

Kambra M.: So, the difference that really makes the difference is that there is the blessing of Grace. Sadguru Kedarji's Blessing—the Shaktipat Blessing. And then there is the Grace and the leadership that Sadguru Kedarji offers. And I compare this to that friend that we can all relate to. That we can all relate to having that one true friend, who, when we are about to make a mistake or we have made a mistake, doesn't hesitate to let us know that we have made a mistake, and offers assistance in correcting us, or helps us learn how not to make that mistake.

And also, helps us see where we are not shining like the bright light that we are, and showing our true nature. So, the leadership that Sadguru Kedarji offers is really like that truest, truest friend—that purest form of friendship you could ever have. And it's all about having that constant, unwavering support in every single moment of every single day along the journey for permanent spiritual transformation.

Interviewer: Thank you. Shanti and Deana, we'll come down the line to you next.

Shanti H.: So, the difference that makes the difference is Grace. And that Grace can only come from a Sadguru. And we are so blessed to have the privilege of a Sadguru right here. And this blessing of Grace gives us the direct experience of the utterances and the teachings that we're taught. And reveals to us our true nature, and heightens our awareness, so that we can see what is really taking place.

And that's what was missing in all of the other spiritual experiences that I've had—was that direct experience. I was just told, you know, this is the teaching, this is the utterance, but I never had a direct experience of it. And that Grace is really what gives that direct experience. And it can only come from a Sadguru.

Deana T.: For me, in my experience, the difference that makes the difference is the awakening of that spiritual awareness. And also, Grace. Grace is my lifeline. As I shared before, I dabbled in a lot of other spiritual paths, and in that dabbling, those two key elements were missing. I had many relaxing, uplifting, energizing experiences, but I never had that direct inner knowing or that awareness—that spiritual awareness. And I certainly never had the experience of Grace extended to me.
No crystal, no meditative visualization of a beach, no tarot card, spirit guide visits, visit to a sacred place ever extended to me that heightened spiritual awareness or that Grace.

Interviewer: Ben and David, is this your experience as well, with the connection to karmas and having authentic Shaktipat, is the difference that makes the difference for you?

Ben T.: Absolutely. Absolutely. I've heard the saying that Grace is the beginning, the middle, and the end. And since receiving Shaktipat, that has been my experience, where Shaktipat is the difference that makes the difference. Prior to receiving Shaktipat, I had looked at several other spiritual paths over time, but there was always something missing in any one of those. I didn't walk away from them with what I really wanted. I didn't—and I never thought that the person who was teaching there was really the right person to be teaching me.

I didn't see that—I didn't have an ongoing experience. There were a lot of words. That changed when I received Shaktipat. Yes, there are ongoing spiritual experiences, but Shaktipat is not just an awakening, an initiation, but it's the beginning, the middle, and the end. It's the entire course of my daily spiritual practices afterwards.

Interviewer: Thank you. David?

David G.: Yes, I would agree that Shaktipat is the difference that makes the difference. I like to think of it like this: my karmas have me facing in a certain direction. And that's the direction I'm going in. And it's towards worldliness. It's towards experiencing whatever I need to experience as a result of my past actions and thoughts. And the way I can turn my head to the left or to the right, and have a spiritually uplifting experience, but eventually, my head comes back to center, and I'm still facing in the same direction that my karmas are taking me. And those spiritually uplifting experiences that I had fade. They become memories, like forgotten dreams. And no matter how much will power I apply, I can't keep my head turned to the right all the time.

Eventually, it comes back to the direction that my karmas are taking me. So, those experiences that I had—turning my head to the left and the right—were glimpses. And what they lacked was the power of Guru's Grace. What Guru's Grace does, is it took my entire karmic direction and shifted it toward spirituality. So instead of facing in the direction it was going before, it's now facing towards spiritual practice, with the aim of merging with my true nature as the Self.

Interviewer: Thank you. This is directed toward Deana, Ben, and David—we'll start with you. How has the receipt of Shaktipat benefitted your spiritual journey and daily life?

David G.: It's completely transformed my life. From when spirituality was a hobby or a distraction, to being my primary focus. In my daily life, I have many, many experiences of stillness, bliss, peace, joy throughout the day. Regardless of what's happening outside of myself, if I remember to turn my attention within, recall the form of my Guru, repeat my mantra, I can instantly experience the same Bliss, Joy, and wonder that I experienced when I received Shaktipat.

Ben T.: Yes, so, I think I said a few minutes ago that prior to receiving Shaktipat, I was not a spiritual person. I didn't even know what spirituality was. After receiving Shaktipat, as I said, I've become a spiritual person from that, and day to day, I don't see a difference now since Shaktipat. The initial awakening. I don't see a difference between the spiritual life and the daily, mundane world. It's all a spiritual path now.

And when obstacles appear—which they inevitably do—in the day-to-day life, that energy inside, coupled with the techniques that I was given when I received Shaktipat, it just punches right through them. And so yes, it makes the daily grind easier, of course. But it also, through the application of those practices, it makes me a better person, overall, every day.

Deana T.: It has literally changed my view of the world, of myself, and everything that I experience. Now I experience more peace and content and happiness for more moments of my day than I used to, and I experience them for no reason. Prior to receiving Shaktipat, I was someone who went about my day, just doing enough to get by. Kind of lazy, looking for praise to avoid being blamed. Living in constant fear. Constant fear of losing my security, my comfort, reward in life.

Fear of confrontation, fear of speaking up, and doing it all while riding that emotional roller coaster. And so, since the receipt of Shaktipat and this blessing of Grace, I'm able to now see these old habits more clearly, and the benefit of that is when I reach for Grace. To imbibe Grace and to live in that state of Grace, I'm able to stop reaching for those bad habits and just experience happiness.

Interviewer: Thank you. Shanti and Kambra, is this the same for you as well? That you're experiencing benefits of Shaktipat in your daily life, and with spiritual practices?

Shanti H.: Absolutely. I know before Shaktipat, I had a very strong victim mentality. Everything was always happening to me. I was always the victim of everything. And I spent my entire life before meeting Sadguru Kedarji suffering from severe depression, which was just fueled by that victim mentality. And after the receipt of Shaktipat, I was able to observe and have the awareness of how much I reach for contracting and binding understandings and tendencies.

Through Sadguru Kedarji's teachings and methods, I have been able to discard those and to let those go, and to stop reaching for them, and to reach for higher understandings, which has had an absolutely tremendous effect on my mental health, my emotional health. I'm experiencing more happiness and peace, and have actually experienced Bliss, which I had thought was just some made up experience.

I never thought it was actually possible, because I suffered so much before meeting Sadguru Kedarji. And really, Shaktipat showed me so much how I cause my own suffering by the understandings that I reach for, and that it is possible to reach for higher understandings and to have a totally different experience as a result.

Kambra M.: The blessing of Shakipat and Guru's Grace is that I am learning how to see how I get in my own way; and how, prior to receiving Shaktipat, I had such a restless mind that I didn't view as a restless mind at all. I thought that I was supposed to always be thinking and always on the go. And so, I'm learning how to have the experience of a quiet mind more and more, and an improved mental state. And as result of reaching for spiritual power more and more often, and on a constant basis, I'm also experiencing more awareness and control over my emotions.

So, I'm calmer, I'm happier, experiencing more peace. Better experiences in all types of relating with all types of people, whether there's a stranger who's yelling at me in the street, or whether I'm being praised for a job well done. So, I really feel so incredibly blessed to be able to experience well-being in all ways, thanks to Shaktipat.

Interviewer: Can you please give me one experience to share with our viewers of receiving Shaktipat from Sadguru Kedarji? Kambra, we'll start with you.

Kambra M.: Thank you. So, I go back to my very first experience of Sadguru Kedarji's Shaktipat Blessing. And at that point in time, I was having difficulty with my back and my spine. I didn't have any flexibility. And when I received Sadguru Kedarji's Shaktipat Blessing, I immediately felt my body relax, and my head went forward and almost touched the ground. So, it was such a beautiful blessing that allowed me to have the direct experience of seeing how I had felt stuck, and how I've limited myself, and how easy it was in an instant to become unstuck. And that it was possible to stay unstuck. So, it was really just an absolutely beautiful experience, and so freeing. And I'm just so, so grateful.

Interviewer: Thank you. Shanti?

Shanti: So, the experience I want to share is actually from our most recent Shaktipat Meditation Retreat. And in this vision during meditation right after Shaktipat, I was standing in front of this massive gorge. And I can only compare it to, like, the Grand Canyon. So, I was standing there with Sadguru Kedarji standing next to me. And He says, "Just step over it. The distance is so small." And I look back at this gorge, this huge canyon, and it's miles and miles across. And I'm like, there's no way I can step over this. I'm so small, and it's so large. I can't.

And Kedarji turns to me again and says, "Just step over it. The distance is so small. And when I looked back again and took the perspective of the Highest, I looked back, and it looked like there was just like a couple of drops of water that had formed a small

streak across the floor. So instead of this huge,
massive canyon, it was just this small little streak
across the floor.

So, from that perspective, I could very easily step
over. And I realized that this analogy, that this canyon
was what I perceived to be the distance between
myself right now and experiencing my true nature on
a constant basis. When I took the view of being just
this person, just this individual, the distance seemed
so vast and so large. But when I take the perspective
of the Highest, and I reach for the Guru's
understandings over my own and look at this, the
distance really is so small and it's so easy to take that
step.

Deana T.: Sure, I'll share my very first Shaktipat
experience, because it was just so wonderful, and
really just filled me with a sense of awe, because I
really didn't know what to expect. I had a very, very
peaceful experience. Prior to receiving Shaktipat, my
mind was very restless. It raced. And then as soon as
the Shaktipat began, my mind slowed down, and then
it stopped. And I was filled with this very peaceful
experience. And in that meditation, I saw an ocean.
And it was just calling to me.

And all I wanted to do was just dive into this ocean
and to be one with it. And, so, I did. And while I was
in this ocean, I had this experience of trying to lift my
hand to see what my hand would be like in this ocean
that I was swimming in. And there was no hand. I
was one with that ocean. I was one with that power.
And then my mind completely dissolved, and I just
drifted off into this beautiful, peaceful experience.
And it was something that I never wanted to end.

Ben T.: Thank you for asking. The experience that I'd like to share was from an intensive. And I was given Shaktipat in that, as were all the other attendees, of course. So, in that, we were asked to sit with straight backs, backs straight, comfortably, and meditate. So, as we were meditating, I was touched on the head and the chest with peacock feathers. And once that happened, I felt a power, a vibration, rippling through my body and my head. And my vision was filled with a light inside. My eyes were still closed. And as I continued to meditate on this, it occurred to me: the realization came to me that what I was experiencing was me.

And that the awakened power inside of me was me, that it was also God. That I was experiencing God inside of myself. And that all of the states, the machinations of the world were my states. They were also God's states. And that the being who gave this to me is Sadguru Kedarji, because it was a gift. I don't think I really did anything in order to receive Shaktipat. But that it was a gift. So that certainly, whoever could provide that gift was also in that state.

David G.: My experience of Shaktipat is being drunk with joy, drunk with Love. My mind stops, and I experience this incredible stillness. But it's not empty. It's very full with Bliss, and a sense of awe and wonder.

**Your Treasure Awaits You.
Why Wait? Claim It Now!**

Just imagine starting at the top rather than the bottom. What is it like to start at the destination, rather than in search of the destination? This is the easy means of authentic Shaktipat.

The gift of *authentic* Shaktipat, full Kundalini Awakening, is transmitted in every weekend Shaktipat Meditation Retreat offered in Nityananda Shaktipat Yoga. Come experience Kedarji's Shaktipat Blessing for yourself. For more information and enrollment visit: https://www.shaktipatblessing.org/.

Chapter 5
Additional Shaktipat
Education Resources

Nityananda Shaktipat Yoga and Kedarji's 4 Pillars of Joy In Daily Living
https://www.nityanandashaktipatyoga.org/.

Chidakasha Gita of Bhagawan Nityananda of Ganeshpuri
This sacred text can be studied here, Free
https://www.nityanandashaktipatyoga.org/about-us-our-approach/wisdom-practices/the-chidakasha-gita/.

Bhagawan Nityananda of Ganeshpuri, By Swami Muktananda Paramahamsa, ISBN 0-911307-45-1. This
sacred text can be purchased here
https://www.amazon.com/.

The Abode of Grace. Bhagawan Nityananda of Ganeshpuri, By Kedarji, ISBN 979-8-218-18009-6. This book can
be purchased here
https://www.nityanandashaktipatyoga.org/the-abode-of-grace-bhagawan-nityananda-of-ganeshpuri/.

Devatma Shakti By Swami Vishnu Tirtha. This sacred
text can be purchased here
https://www.amazon.com/.

Shiva Sutras of Lord Shiva – The Yoga of Supreme Identity, With Translation and Commentary By Jaideva Singh, ISBN
978-81-208-0407-4. This sacred text can be purchased
here
https://yoursacredstore.org/sacred-texts/.

Vibration of Divine Consciousness – A Spiritual

Autobiography By Kedarji, ISBN 978-0-595-27410-9. This sacred text can be purchased here https://www.nityanandashaktipatyoga.org/vibration-of-divine-consciousness/.

The Verses On Witness Consciousness By Kedarji, ISBN 978-0-692-74115-3. This sacred text can be purchased here https://www.nityanandashaktipatyoga.org/the-verses-on-witness-consciousness/.

13 QUESTIONS TO ASK *BEFORE* YOU CONSIDER RECEIVING SHAKTIPAT FROM ANYONE – **Answers that apply to Kedarji and Nityananda Shaktipat Yoga**

1. Who is your Guru?

Muktananda Paramahamsa. Before his passing, Muktananda told Kedarji that Kedarji's God-realization was immanent, and that he should begin meditating on Bhagawan Nityananda of Ganeshpuri. Kedarji was also told that he should follow every inner command Bhagawan Nityananda gives him. This is how we have this offering, named after Bhagawan Nityananda of Ganeshpuri, the master of our lineage in these modern times and a world renown Avadhut.

2. How long did you or have you served your Guru?

Kedarji served his Guru in ashrams and centers for 18.5 years. This period corresponds to the period of his Sadhana under his Guru's leadership. He continues to serve his Guru to this day.

3. How much time did you/do you spend in the company of your Guru each month?

During his Sadhana and service under his Guru's leadership, Kedarji spent an average of 4-6 days per week, each and every week, in his Guru's ashrams and centers. This time was taken up in attending programs, performing selfless service and keeping the company of his Guru. In addition, Kedarji participated in joining and supporting the world tours of his Guru and the successors to his Guru's foundation. All of this occurred during the 18.5 years mentioned above.

4. What is your feeling for your Guru?

Even though his Guru is no longer in physical form, Kedarji's Love and Longing for his Guru is evident in his many talks and writings in which he also quotes his Guru regularly. This love for his Guru is also a common observation on the part of his devotees and disciples. Kedarji never stops talking about his Guru and has said that he is just a puppet – that it is his Guru who has taken up residence in him, leading our mission.

5. Were you accepted as a Disciple of your Guru?
Yes, after making a request for Discipleship, Kedarji was accepted as a disciple.

6. Did your Guru have a Guru who he/she served for an extended period of time as a Disciple?
Yes. Bhagawan Nityananda of Ganeshpuri.

7. How did your Guru receive the authorization to give Shaktipat?
Bhagawan Nityananda built an ashram for Kedarji's Guru. He then began sending devotees to Muktananda Baba. Muktananda received both an outer and inner command from Bhagawan Nityananda to give Shaktipat.

8. How did you receive the authorization to give Shaktipat and when were you authorized?
Kedarji received the authorization to give Shaktipat in the form of his Guru's final words to him that his God-realization was immanent. That occurred in 1981. He then received the authorization again as an inner command from Bhagawan Nityananda, Muktananda Paramahamsa and Lord Shiva. That command came in 1996. The power of Kedarji to transmit authentic Shaktipat has been verified by a good number of people who received Shaktipat from

his Guru and other Shaktipat Gurus in our lineage.

9. Do you have any written documentation or something other than a picture that shows that you had/have a Guru and that you served that Guru for an extended period of time?

Yes. There are several notes/letters that provide evidence of this fact. These can be viewed, by appointment, in the office of our school. The reason we don't post these online is to avoid the hacking, reproduction and altering of the copyrighted material on our web sites that has occurred in the past.

10. Or are there other people who also served your Guru in the period that you did, who can verify that you did so?

Yes. There are people, both in our spiritual community and at large, who were present when Kedarji performed his service to his Guru and have verified that this occurred. These are people who followed his Guru and/or the successors to his Guru's foundation.

11. Do you have video testimonials at your web site from people who have received Shaktipat from you?

Yes. You can view these videos on this page. https://www.shaktipatblessing.org/shaktipat-experiences/.

12. Are some of those people available to speak to me directly about their experience?

Yes. Most of the people interviewed for the videos participate in our spiritual community. Arrangements can be made to make contact with them, upon request.

13. After giving Shaktipat, what support do you provide in the form of programs, course of study and leadership to nurture the unfolding of the awakened Kundalini?

Nityananda Shaktipat Yoga is a curriculum that is part of our school – The Bhakta School of Transformation – our not-for-profit public charity. So, we are a school where the full support necessary for nurturing the fully awakened Kundalini is offered year-round. Go here for more information. https://www.nityanandashaktipatyoga.org/.